Color in the Garden

Planting with Color in the Contemporary garden

for Chloe and Emily

For the UK edition: **Commissioning Editor** Stuart Cooper **Managing Editor** Richard Atkinson **Copy Editor** Liz Robinson

Art Director Leslie Harrington **Art Editor** Vanessa Courtier **Photographic Art Direction** Vanessa Courtier **Production** Jill Beed and Suzanne Sharpless

For SOMA edition: **Publisher** James Connolly **Art Director** Jeffrey O'Rourke **Managing Editor** Clancy Drake **North American Editor** Melinda Levine **Production** Jeff Brandenburg

Text © Nori and Sandra Pope 1998. Photographs © Clive Nichols 1998. Design and layout © Conran Octopus Limited 1998. North American text © SOMA Books 1998.

First published in 1998 by Conran Octopus Limited. North American hardcover edition published 1998 by SOMA Books, by arrangement with Conran Octopus Limited.

North American paperback edition, titled Colour in the Garden, published 2002 by SOMA Books by arrangement with Conran Octopus Limited.

SOMA Books is an imprint of Bay/SOMA Publishing, 444 De Haro St, No. 130, San Francisco, CA 94107

Library of Congress Cataloguing –in –Publication Data

Pope, Nori. Color by Design : Planting the contemporary garden / Nori and Sandra Pope ; forward by Penelope Hob house ; photography by Clive Nichols. P. cm. Includes index.

ISBN 1-57959-076-4 1. Color in gardening. 2. Gardens—Design. I. Pope, Sandra. II. Title. SB454.3.C64P67 1998 712—dc21 98-3891 CIP

Distributed to the trade by Publishers Group West Printed in China 10 9 8 7 6 5 4 3 2 1

Nori and Sandra Pope

Color in the Garden

Planting with Color in the Contemporary garden

foreword by Penelope Hobhouse   photography by Clive Nichols

SOMA
san francisco

contents

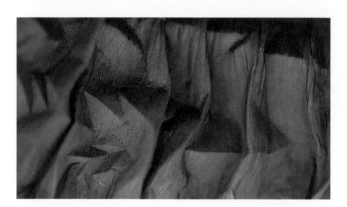

GREEN 32 – 45

YELLOW 46 – 61

RED 78 – 93

PLUM 94 – 107

PEACH 124 – 137

WHITE 138 – 149

Nori and Sandra Pope have made Hadspen Garden, in Somerset, England, a place of pilgrimage for all those interested in designing with color. Now they have given us a book which, drawing on their own unique plant wisdom and experience, amplifies their schemes and extends our understanding of the drama of color and its effect on mood.

The use of color in the garden remains highly emotive and subjective. Do we emphasize contrasts for visual stimulation, or go for well-tried harmonies of spectral hues? The Popes, although aware of the extra excitement achieved by adding a touch of blue to a yellow border, love to trace nuances of shared pigment in spectral harmonies. In the borders at Hadspen, warmer colors — oranges, scarlets, deep reds — flow into darker crimsons, set off by purple or bronze foliage; and azure blues fade to velvety violets, with paler colors following similar patterns. This is, of course, a simplification: it is the artist-gardener who knows how to plan and who understands how colors placed together will alter and affect each other, holding these color memories in the mind's eye when planning border schemes and carefully preparing color sequences that will unfold through the seven months of an English summer.

As the Popes say in their own introduction, gardening with color is a means of personal expression. Previously we could share the visual results of their philosophy only by visiting Hadspen, but now we can follow the intricate details of their development as color specialists and, thanks to Clive Nichols's superb photographs, we can compare science with reality. Having once lived at Hadspen — leaving nearly ten years before the Popes arrived as gardeners — I find it exhilarating to return to find the walled garden so beautiful. I treasure my friendship with Sandra and Nori and am thrilled to learn their color philosophy.

Penelope Hobhouse
Bettiscombe, Dorset
England

introduction

This book is about how and why we garden with color, not about how we made a garden. It is about the pursuit of gardening as a means of expression. Our garden is an accurate reflection of ourselves, and of how we interface with the natural world; it is intensely entangled with our aesthetic lives. In no way is our garden a low-maintenance or frugal affair.

There has never been a better time to garden, with a plethora of plants being fed into the gardening world by botanists, plant hunters and breeders, and with education, communication and travel broadening both knowledge and expectation. Through our writing, we hope to share our gardening philosophy and our techniques, and to inspire people to use all the tools so ready at hand.

William Robinson wrote in *The English Flower Garden and Home Grounds* in 1883: "One of the most important points in the arrangement of a garden is the placing of the flowers with regard to their color-effect. Too often a garden is an assemblage of plants placed together haphazard, or if any intention be perceptible, as is commonly the case in the bedding system, it is to obtain as great a number as possible of the most violent contrasts; and the result is a hard, garish vulgarity. Then, in mixed borders, one usually sees lines or evenly distributed spots of color, wearying and annoying to the eye, and proving how poor an effect can be got by the misuse of the best materials. Should it not be remembered that in setting a garden we are painting — a picture of hundreds of feet or yards instead of so many inches, painted with living flowers and seen by open daylight — so

that to paint it rightly is a debt that we owe to the beauty of flowers and to the light of the sun; that the colors should be placed with careful forethought and deliberation as a painter employs them on his picture, and not dropped down in lifeless daubs. Harmony rather than contrast — splendid harmonies of rich and brilliant color, and proper sequences of such harmonies, should be the rule."

Color surrounds us, often confounds us. Never before has such a wide range of varied colors, both pure and impure, been so universally available, in paints and in fabric — and in plants. As we look around, great slabs of color, often far from subtle in hue, tumble over one another, on signs, on automobiles, in gardens, everywhere — a cacophony of color noise. A passion for color at its finest, combined with excitement about the effect it has on perception and emotion, have become the basis for our design at Hadspen Garden.

For centuries people have tried to systematize the use of color. Complex configurations have been worked out in an attempt to connect the physics of light with the perception of color. As scientists and others came to understand more, they began to realize that light waves themselves are not colored, but that color arises in the brain and is discriminated by the eye. The great German poet Goethe tried to relate the wavelengths of sound in music to the wavelengths of color, even going so far as to represent pure blue as the note G below middle C. This idea appeals enormously to us, but we lean entirely toward a subjective interpretation.

One of the most widely used devices for representing the perception of visible light is the color wheel in its simplest form, conventionally divided into solid blocks of red, orange, yellow, green, blue, indigo and violet — the seven colors of the rainbow. It was first introduced by the mathematician Sir Isaac Newton, who in 1672 presented his new theory about light and colors to the Royal Society. Here he described how, in the course of his experiments, he had noted that a beam of sunlight passing through a prism formed a band of colors like a rainbow. The division of this band into seven colors is purely arbitrary — though it accorded well with the theories of Newton's day regarding the unity of all things: the seven days of Creation, the seven known planets, the seven-tone musical scale. In fact, of course, each color as actually perceived by the eye shades gradually into another, as the notes making up a chord blend harmoniously when played on the cello.

Over the last twenty years or so the use of contrast above all else has been widely advocated: each plant must contrast with its neighbour in color, size and shape. If continual contrasts were exciting, mixed busy-lizzies would be the best thing to use — but they are not. Yellow with magenta is a clap of cymbals: once is exciting, twice is tolerable, but by the third, you wish it would just stop. Would Elgar's Concerto in E minor be the better for a few contrasting keys? As a system of creating dramatic tension, increasing perception and manipulating mood change, we advocate planting in a developing monochrome. Less is more: by using monochrome (single-color) plantings at Hadspen, we can closely control the color shift, the saturation of color and the tonal change from dark to light. Using a single color also makes it possible to focus on foliage and on flower shapes, on the rhythm and structure of the planting and, of course, on the full impact of what the color offers emotionally. A border of yellow gives a sense of enlightenment, like a shaft of sunlight coming through a window. Combine this same yellow with a small amount of blue, and the experience changes: the yellow still projects the light, while the blue withdraws, enhancing the yellow even more. Alter the balance of the planting by making blue the dominant color for yet another picture, and for a whole shift of emotional experience.

Foliage, too, plays an important role. A strong metallic-bronze leaf will give a sobering quality to a planting, compared to green or yellow foliage. The grays of lavender, artemisia or dianthus teamed with pastel shades give a Mediterranean effect. What better foliage is there than that provided by many vegetables? Ruby chard can compare with the rarest hosta, and the common leek is a subtle gray lance. All are of use in the border — but why stop there? Even more fun are the blocks of pattern, texture and color that can be created with vegetables in a kitchen garden.

Color often dictates where and how it must be placed. Since saturated red cannot be seen at a distance (as you move farther away, it becomes increasingly black — especially for men), placing it at the far end of a garden makes little sense. At one yard red sings; at three yards, it is still pretty sonorous; at fifty, it is hard to differentiate from dark green shadows. Everyone knows that red reads in your face — and that is a very good place for it. Just as distant hills always seem shrouded in gray-blue, a path edged with this distant hue will run on in the mind's eye.

People often ask us, in an amazed way, "How do you possibly garden together?" — yet they never stop to question a couple playing a duet. Like a flute and a cello playing together, one person's strengths fill in for the other's weaknesses. The human eye contains two kinds of receptors: rods respond to light or darkness; cones are sensitive to color and detail. Men's eyes have more rods, a thousand times more sensitive to light than cones, so men wait for low light, often seeing better in the dark. With a plethora of cones, women may stumble in the dark but are better able to respond to the subtle blush of a rose. It doesn't stop there. Men and women process the information that comes in through their eyes differently. Women store visual information on both sides of their brain, men on one side only: this gives men better depth perception, but at the price of color recall, which is easier for women. Ten percent of men are functionally color blind, and almost none have the selective capacity of a woman's eye, well trained. In November, when I am planting bulbs, I can rely on Sandra to recall just the violet shade of *Tulipa* 'Greuze', and whether it will sing with *Dicentra spectabilis* 'Goldheart'. Few great gardens have been made by only one person — I can think of none.

In garden planning as in other forms of design — interior, fashion, industrial — color is one of the most dominant aspects, and with so many colors available in so many forms, an awareness of color and how it affects our lives is more important today than it has ever been before. In this book we emphasize the strength and power of color, but also stress the other elements of design, exploring shape, form, texture and rhythm. So often people will take great care with color in what they wear or the rooms they live in, but somehow never think to extend any sense of style to the garden — yet a moment of thought given to a plant combination can make the difference between pleasure at the result, or disgust.

An important aspect of any planting at Hadspen is that it must perform for at least seven months of the year, maintaining not just the color of the area but also the general ambience, the rhythm and the mood — to create a picture that may change from season to season in form, but not in content. Unlike the borders of Gertrude Jekyll, who used to close off certain plantings once their time was up, the borders here keep working

THE BLUE-SILVER TONE OF *CERINTHE MAJOR* 'PURPURASCENS' EXUDES THE OMINOUS ATMOSPHERE OF PREDAWN LIGHT, BENDING AWAY FROM TRUE BLUE IN BOTH TONE AND HUE WITH THE SAME SENSUAL TWIST THAT COLTRANE MANAGES TO PULL FROM AN F-SHARP.

through the seasons. The tulip 'Red Shine' is replaced by *Papaver orientale* 'Beauty of Livermere', which is followed by the dahlia 'Bishop of Llandaff'. Once the poppies are finished, they are cut to the ground; annuals or half-hardy perennials are planted close in; and the poppy foliage sprouts up again around them. *Phlox, Saponaria* and *Lychnis* are pinched out by a third in April to stagger their flowering and encourage them to continue over months instead of weeks. Every visible sliver of earth is planted with bulbs, perennials, annuals, shrubs and climbers. Weeds can seize no foothold in this exuberance, and for seven months every year the concert continues.

We did not come to color from a vacuum. In our Canadian garden by the Tsolum River on Vancouver Island, British Columbia, we devoured Gertrude Jekyll's *Color Schemes for the Flower Garden* and Penelope Hobhouse's *Color in Your Garden*. In 1986 we came to England, the Mecca of twentieth-century gardening, and while travelling in the southwest of the country we came upon Hadspen, in Somerset. After many years of neglect the garden was a ghost of itself. Saplings grew through the paths; ivy and brambles ruled what once had been walls and borders; huge rambling roses hung in the trees. This was no carte blanche canvas, but a romantic frame waiting for a painting. We did not know we were looking for this until we found it, and having done so, we upped stakes and moved halfway around the world. Who could resist the crumbling walled garden, the ancient huts, the dank cistern? The historical context — just what we had not had as a backdrop for our work in the Pacific Northwest — was an undeniable attraction: the garden walls were built before Canada was a country, and we find the atmosphere they create as alluring and enchanting today as when we first saw it.

Hadspen certainly provides a utopian setting for our work. It is a classic eighteenth-century country estate of elegant Georgian manor house, pretty cottages, stables and a walled kitchen garden, all surrounded by grazed fields and mature deciduous woodlands. In 1759 a visitor to Hadspen House wrote: "We were gratified with the sight of a very handsome house, low, wide, regularly built of a yellowish sort of stone, before which was a very long and wide lawn rather descending, and to the left of the house a fine high wood."

IN CLOSE-UP THE SUBJECT BECOMES ABSTRACT AND WE BEGIN TO UNDERSTAND ITS COLOR AND THE MEANING OF ITS STRUCTURE. THE INHERENT DIFFERENCES BETWEEN RUBY CHARD AND MALACHITE BECOME BLURRED WHEN THEIR INNERMOST COLOR IS THUS REVEALED.

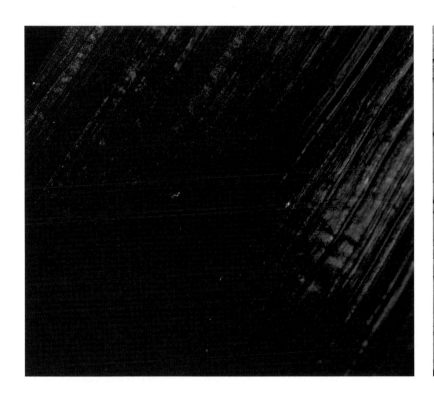
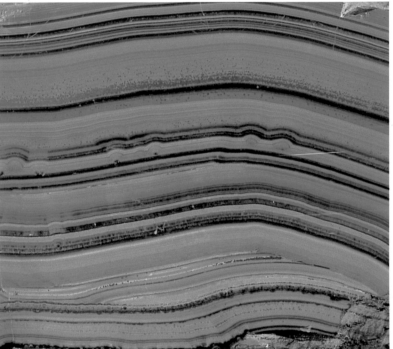

When we arrived here, the scene had already long since been set for a continuing embellishment of the grounds. Margaret Hobhouse had come in 1880 as a young bride, laden with plants from her family home to grace her new garden. She carried on developing the garden with enthusiasm, planting many good trees and shrubs and creating a meadow and parkland area in the William Robinson style. After her reign, years of neglect and decay followed, a not unusual occurrence with estates such as this — a result of the financial and social upheavals following the First and Second World Wars. Then in the 1960s, Paul and Penelope Hobhouse came to live here, and for a period of twelve years, the garden flourished again in Penelope's hands.

Penelope Hobhouse had the foresight to hire Eric Smith, formerly of Buckshaw Nursery in Dorset, one of England's great plantsmen and a plant breeder of international repute. So many new *Hosta*, *Hellebore* and *Kniphofia* varieties came from a small strip of land in the kitchen garden that Hadspen was put firmly on the gardening map. Plants from Hadspen found their way into gardens all over the United Kingdom, and to North

America and New Zealand. One of Eric's culinary delights was comfrey (*Symphytum × uplandicum*), and when he and Penelope were no longer there, the garden fell again into neglect, and grew ever wilder; the comfrey grew wilder still. Years later, when the garden had returned to nature, the comfrey survived as a reminder of those days.

Hadspen Garden, as this part of the estate is known today, is set in the original kitchen garden belonging to the house, a superb south-facing site encircled by a hillside of mature woodland. The soil is unenviable, a heavy alkaline clay — the bricks used in the construction of the earliest walls are reputed to have been made on site. The garden, of about five acres, is now approached through the utilitarian entrance of the potting shed and nursery. Victorian masons were responsible for two dramatic southern terraces. The lower one incorporates a large brick and stone cistern, now a lily pond, while the upper terrace leads to a thicket of trees, a wooded glade, which hides the old gardener's cottage, now the teahouse. The D-shape of the original walled garden is a unique and interesting design, its structure a quite astonishing engineering feat. Situated on a south-facing slope, the wall curves down the slope to allow for air drainage and thus creates a microclimate within it, while the strength of its shape ensures its stability on the slippery clay soil beneath — and it was all devised by a local builder, several hundred years ago. The wall encloses about 2½ acres, originally given over entirely to the production of fruit and vegetables. Here we are able to indulge to the full our passion for color, using herbaceous plants, roses, shrubs and still, of course, fruit and vegetables. The space is divided into four parts by two paths. From the main door one path cuts straight ahead through a deep double border backed by a beech hedge, leading to a gate and a view that takes the eye up the surrounding hill to the distant skyline. The crosspath, lined with a double row of *Nepeta* 'Six Hills Giant', leads to a bench beneath a clematis-covered arbor at one end, and out into a wildflower meadow at the other. The curved wall backs a deep border and path that run the whole 820 yards of its length, passing from the hottest, most well-drained spot in the garden to the coolest and shadiest. Within the curve of the D, vegetables are grown in an intensive organic system in rectangular beds about 1 yard wide (from the paths we can just reach past the middles, to weed and to plant) and 3 yards long. The regimented patterns of these vegetables contrast texturally with the overflowing exuberance of the borders they parallel. The straight part of the D provides a north-facing elevation for hydrangeas, the National *Rodgersia* Collection, and other woodlanders. These mainly foliage plantings lead out into the meadow, and connect the garden to the woodland beyond.

The functional layout of the walls in our garden has had little to do with any aesthetic contrivance; there is no diminishing perspective, no alignment, whether of doorways or of water-filled reflective brooks. But all pictures have a frame, and ours is provided by the many hues of crumbling brick walls — pale buff terracotta in some areas, overfired, almost iridescent plum in others. The newest, harsh red Victorian walls reveal in their large, dangerous cracks the arrogance or ignorance of the men who built them, using newfangled hard cement mortar instead of the old-fashioned soft lime-based mortar that could accommodate itself to structural movement. The key to everything lay in that curved wall, approximately 9 feet high with a slightly wider border at its foot, and 820 yards long. That first cold January in 1987, the plum-toned bricks, like a single opening note on a cello, told us where to begin; we now knew where the plum border would start, and so had committed ourselves to the nature of our work. For years we had admired the rich, intricate patterns of the Shiraz rugs of central Persia, which were derived from garden plans, and had wanted to reinterpret them in a modern planting. This change-of-medium approach has always been appealing — planting a piece of music, painting a garden, knitting a border. Having made one choice, the next became easier. In one direction the wall curves away uphill, changing from plum to an Umbrian orange: we drew the color up from plum, through the reds, to meet the orange. Each flower was chosen to move toward a more pure hue, of red and then orange, and gradually we raised the tone of the petal-color while maintaining the darkness of the leaf coloring, the bass notes of the leaves integrating the higher harmonies. The corresponding long curve of the wall in the opposite direction made it natural then to extend this progression of colors from the simplicity of whole tones in the upper half of the curve to the complexities of pastel half-tones in the lower half. A door nearly in the center of the wall marks an axis and presents the obvious place to slip into the other side of the mirror image. The complicated mixtures of magentas, peaches and apricots can be seen from the upper path, and being half-toned pastels can be read at a great distance. Wherever possible we strive to move from light to dark, short to tall, pale to saturated, with the monochrome rhythm driving the composition forward. Yet always the habitat will influence the design: a low corner suits *Rodgersia* or *Rheum*, and the huge dark leaves are tied into the picture by a thread of color drawn from the connecting border.

THE TRANSCENDENTAL, OPALESCENT QUALITY OF MOTHER-OF-PEARL, SEEN ALSO IN *NECTAROSCORDUM*, HAS SUCH UNIVERSAL APPEAL THAT IT MUST BE CONNECTED DIRECTLY TO OUR INNERMOST PSYCHE.

Our garden is just larger than the two of us can manage by ourselves, which saves it from being overworked or overtidied — that overzealousness that spells death to so many gardens, as it does to paintings. In *A Gentle Plea For Chaos*, as Mirabel Osler so eloquently points out, ". . . when I make a plea for havoc, what would be lost? Merely the pristine appearance of a garden kept highly manicured, which could be squandered for amiable disorder. Just in some places. Just to give a pull at our primeval senses. A mild desire for amorphous confusion which will gently infiltrate and, given time, will one day set the garden singing."

Traveled, educated and increasingly demanding, people garden today more than ever before, and one of the dominant characteristics of gardens of the late-twentieth century is that they are singularly private and individual works of art. They are gardens both designed and worked by their owners, fine-tuned day by day, every nuance of light and situation studied and taken into consideration. Such gardens are most readily comparable to what is produced by the painters and musicians of this egalitarian century. In England the gardens of the Healings at the Priory, Kemerton, Worcestershire; the Lewises at Sticky Wicket, Buckland Newton, Dorset; and the Perrys at Bosvigo House, Truro, Cornwall are continual sources of inspiration. Their makers are always pushing forward the leading edge of what it is possible to achieve using color. Neocolorists have been at work throughout the twentieth century, but are concentrated in this final decade.

The act of looking is, of course, a personal activity and ability, but there are always things to be learned to enhance it. We are fortunate that painters, musicians, designers and photographers visit Hadspen, and share their experience of it with us: we learn so much from their different points of view, their educated impressions. Inasmuch as gardening is an art, it is one we are trying to communicate, and we achieve success if visitors enjoy the garden. Over the several years Clive Nichols has been photographing our work, he has shared his vision with us and become in turn an inspiration. This book allows us the opportunity to explore our use of color in gardening through the visionary interpretation of Clive's photography.

Hadspen Garden, Somerset, England
February 1998

THIS PLAN OF HADSPEN GARDEN SHOWS
THE LAYOUT OF THE COLOR-THEMED
BORDERS WITHIN THE OLD KITCHEN
GARDEN INCLUDING THE MEDITERRANEAN
WALK ABOVE THE LILY POND, THE BLUE
GARDEN AT THE TEAHOUSE AND THE
UNIQUE DESIGN OF THE D-SHAPED WALL
PROTECTING THE LONG BORDERS AND
THE KITCHEN GARDEN FROM FROSTS.

N

BLUE at its most

rarely, and it is possibly this rarity that has led people to seek it; that it is rarely attained makes it all the more desirable. Baby pharaohs were swaddled in blue to indicate their celestial nature, and for the Chinese, blue was the color of the transcendental path to immortality. Grindings of costly lapis lazuli were used in icons for the robes of the Virgin Mary throughout the Middle Ages. This precious color came to represent both the Virgin Mary and the power and wealth of the church of the day. Blue dyes have long been sought for religious and commercial purposes, and two dye plants grown for thousands of years — woad (*Isatis tinctoria*) and indigo (*Indigofera tinctoria*) — are to be seen in many gardens. Indigo-dyed textiles have been found in Egyptian tombs, and the demand for blue has spread the cultivation of such plants as indigo around the world. As much wealth and energy have probably also been invested in seeking out blue-flowered plants to embellish the garden, from the absurd folly of a blue rose to the purest-hued delphinium.

All colors can vary in several directions. Blue can vary in hue, to be more greenish or more reddish; it can vary in saturation, to appear more or less watery; it can vary in brilliance, as it is more or less diluted with white or black; and it can vary in effect, for example, when it is surrounded by orange, its complementary color. It is common knowledge that blue is a cool color and red, a warm one. This is partly the effect of association — the heat of a red fire, the chill of blue shadows on snow — but also literally true. Paint a flat piece of metal pure blue and another pure red, and set both in the sun for a few minutes: placing a hand on each, you will notice at once that the red is warmer to the touch. Why? Because blue absorbs less light than red does (light is energy, and when absorbed, becomes heat).

true is found in nature but

Planting with color is like making music. Just as in music, there are harmonic intervals in which each note has a special relationship to every other, so in our plantings, each tonal change must be governed by the power of its nearest neighbour and the way it alters the whole piece. Within blue there are more divergences from the pure color than not, more notes of discord. It would be possible to plant John Coltrane's Lazy Bird using the dissonances of blue, but I would need the major key of yellow for Mahler's Second Symphony.

The color of unreachable horizons, blue also represents the coolness of withdrawal, both visually (blue objects always appear more distant) and emotionally (I feel blue, we sing the blues). Blue is remote, constrained. There is no passion in blue: it is the color of the pinstriped suit of power and reason, of refined and confident contemplation.

We all live in two worlds — the world of science, of objects and solidity; and the world of dreams, of patterns and rhythms of color and sound. Gardening is a synthesis of these two worlds, of object and illusion. In *The Elements of Color*, the Swiss color theorist Johannes Itten says that blue is "a power like that of nature in winter, when all germination and growth is hidden in darkness and silence." Blue is a building block, the primary color from which we begin to construct the complexity of our color world, and Matisse says that, "Given a correct fundamental attitude, it would turn out that the procedure of making a 'picture' garden is no less logical than that of building a house." It is important to remember, when confronted and possibly dazzled by the apparent complexities of planting with color, that after all you are only making a garden: mistakes are permitted, and will harm no one. They might even be fun.

'PERLE D'AZUR' IS THE BLUEST CLEMATIS
WE KNOW; TYING IN THE GROWING
SHOOTS HORIZONTALLY WILL CAUSE
MANY MORE FLOWERS TO FORM.
WHITE DOTS OF *GYPSOPHILA PANICULATA*
'BRISTOL FAIRY' (BABY'S-BREATH) LIFT
THE DEEP COLOR OF *CERINTHE MAJOR*
'PURPURASCENS'. AGAPANTHUS, GLIMPSED
HERE STILL IN BUD, WILL FORM THE
BACKBONE OF LATE SUMMER'S BLUES.

Using blue

Blue carries a different charge for temperate-climate gardeners than it does for those living in more tropical regions. The clear-blue sky of spring holds another message for the blue-robed Bedouins of the Sahara or the Masai herdsmen of the African veld: they would not seek that blue sky, but rather avoid it. Part of our own deep reaction to the color is surely to do with dreaming through winter of *Chionodoxa* (glory-of-the-snow) days. Blue looks great in the thin spring light: what a good thing there is so much of it available at this time of year.

In our planting of blue at Hadspen, we try to hold on to the ambiguity between the cool of Cambridge blue and the warmth of indigo. One hue away from green, the foliage of a blue planting can easily be slipped over into the haze between the two. Blue sits easily in the landscape because it is so close to the main field color of green, but although blue is cool, a drop of red finds its way into almost all shades — lavender, indigo, violet — and a red center makes a good target for bees, which see more clearly in the ultraviolet range.

Tadao Ando, the great Japanese modern architect, has said: "Geometry is a symbol of reason as opposed to the state of nature. That is, geometry is the stamp that shows gardening is the expression of human will and not a product of nature." The eye tends to follow light, repeating colors, shapes or patterns — for example, it will connect a nigella in the foreground to one in the middle ground, and so on into the distance. This fact provides a tool with which to control a garden's audience, to draw and direct movement through the garden, much as an architect will direct the flow of movement around a building by making the feet follow the eyes. A rounded shape — a mound of, say, *Geranium* 'Johnson's Blue' — will stop the eye, and therefore the feet, and so encourage an intense examination of the surrounding detail.

Although it is, of course, the linked similarities that create a feeling of single-mindedness in a planting, "the best associations are always between plants which have an element in common and one in contrast," as Dame Sylvia Crowe wrote in *Garden Design*. The beard of

Iris 'Blue Sapphire' can be counted on to match the contrasting stamens of *Campanula cochleariifolia* or even *Ceanothus* 'Puget Blue'; the pale eye of *Geranium wallichianum* 'Buxton's Variety' looks up to the pale lip of *Lobelia siphilitica*, the very difference between their flowers uniting them.

The most important aspect of using blue in design is its ability to drop back in a picture, causing even a wall to recede. Bluebells stretching off under trees draw the eye to the horizon, and the blueness increases the feeling of spaciousness. In the garden, blue, used to create visual shadows, accentuates the three-dimensional quality. The small dots of *Geranium pratense* used in our yellow border in summer add disproportionately to its sculptural shaping as the blue dots seem to sink into the background; a side effect is that the violet-blue provides an exaggerated simultaneous contrast with the yellow, turning up the volume of our perception of it. Wendy Perry of Bosvigo House in Cornwall, England, another colorist gardener, also uses blue to create the effect of shadows, but in broad-brush rather than in a pointillist way.

Here *Corydalis flexuosa* 'Purple Leaf', an exact color match with the red flowers and the russet fuzz on the leaves of *Rhododendron* 'Loch Heart' as seen in real shade, is planted as its shadow. Impressionists would delight in the effect of a blue shadow of *Camassia leichtlinii* beneath the orange-yellow azalea 'Cécile Grant'. Although Wendy Perry claims not to plant in monochrome, *Ceanothus* 'Concha' overgrown with *Clematis* x *durandii* and fronted by a tangle of *Ceratostigma willmottianum* and *Teucrium fruticans* make a harmonious medley in her garden.

The mountains of Mexico, Brazil and Paraguay have provided some of the most intensely blue flowers for use late in the season. Salvias are one of the few genera to have representatives in all colors, and they are in the most extreme, saturated shades. If a blue can dazzle, it is the blue of *Salvia patens*, while *S. guaranitica*, like an electric spark, short-circuits any thought of the subdued. The sight of *S. patens* 'Guanajuato', whether in an English garden or a creek bed in its native Mexico, would light up anyone's desire for it. The European and North African salvias

left THE FLAT WHITE BELLS OF *CAMPANULA PERSICIFOLIA ALBA* MAKE A RELIABLY FLORIFEROUS CLUMP IN FRONT OF THE LONG-FLOWERING *NEPETA* 'SIX HILLS GIANT', WHOSE INDIVIDUALLY INSIGNIFICANT FLOWERS MAKE A GOOD SETTING FOR THE CRISP OUTLINE OF *CAMPANULA*. A LIGHT SHEARING AFTER THE FIRST FLUSH OF BLOOM WILL ENCOURAGE THIS *NEPETA* TO FLOWER AGAIN, INTO OCTOBER.

right WITH ITS GLAUCOUS LEAVES, INTENSE INDIGO BELL-SHAPED BRACTS AND ULTRAVIOLET FLOWERS, IT IS WITH GOOD REASON THAT THIS EASY MEDITERRANEAN NATIVE, *CERINTHE MAJOR* 'PURPURASCENS', HAS BECOME SO POPULAR. THE SPINY BLUE BRACTS AND LEAVES OF *ERYNGIUM X OLIVERIANUM*, WITH ITS THORNY THIMBLE CENTERS, ARE IN PERFECT TEXTURAL CONTRAST TO THE FLESHY *CERINTHE* LEAVES.

left *IRIS GERMANICA* 'BLUE SAPPHIRE' IS THE PLANT IRIS DREAMS ARE MADE OF. ON A PLANT 3 FOOT HIGH, ALL THE SCULPTURAL QUALITY OF AN ICE CARVING IS BROUGHT TO LIFE IN THE TISSUELIKE STRUCTURE OF PERFECT EPHEMERAL SEE-THROUGH BLUE FLOWERS. NOTE AS WELL THE CONCENTRATED COLOR OF THE BUDS, AND THE SOLIDITY OF THE SHAPE.

right *NIGELLA DAMASCENA* 'MISS JEKYLL' IS OUR MOST VALUED BLUE SELF-SEEDER. A SUCCESSION OF PLANTS WITH THEIR CHARACTERISTIC FILAMENTAL GROWTH AND BACHELOR'S-BUTTON-BLUE FLOWERS CAN BE HAD BY KEEPING SOME OF THE SEED FROM THE YEAR BEFORE AND SCATTERING IT WHERE YOU WILL EVERY FOUR OR FIVE WEEKS IN SPRING AND EARLY SUMMER. THE HANDSOME SEEDPODS LAST WELL INTO WINTER.

sing a softer blue note and often combine several tonal changes in the same flower. For subtle combinations of pastel blues and violet, there is *S. pratensis* Haematodes Group, or *S. sclarea* var. *turkestanica*, particularly in the fine form reintroduced by Dr. James Compton. *Salvia patens* has flowers that are impossibly blue, as unreal as pieces of the sky.

At Hadspen we have used blue in our only garden room, the tea garden where visitors stop to sit and sip and have a sandwich. It is a cool pool in the storm of ferocious color, a simple rectangular layout prompting a relaxed and uncomplicated reaction. The alignment is straightforward, to maximize the sense of peace, and the blue planting overflows to blur the edges and give the feeling of nature taking over: *Geranium* 'Johnson's Blue' with *Cerinthe major* 'Purpurascens' and *Ceratostigma willmottianum*, *Baptisia australis* pushing through carpets of *Borago laxiflora*, and self-seeded *Nigella damascena* 'Miss Jekyll' filling every crack, all tangled together in a seemingly unstudied and haphazard way. In this mood we want the stillness to be the essence. By keeping to

small flowers, sprays of blue dots with fine foliage rather than anything large or flashy, we can create a scene, a matrix, as tightly woven as a piece of fabric, as subdued as a length of tweed.

Since blue leaves are on the border between gray and green, they could as well be discussed in the white chapter, which also encompasses silver and gray. Such shades might be used to set up a beautiful harmony, using the blue of *Iris sibirica* 'Perry's Blue' with *Hosta* 'Hadspen Blue' or 'Blue Wedgwood', the green-blue flash of the iris standards linking with the hosta leaves. It is just such an equilibrium that we seek to achieve here: the visual weight of *Clematis* 'Perle d'Azur' bent and tied to balance with that of *Ceanothus × delilianus* 'Gloire de Versailles', the trees beyond and then the sky, the garden extended to forever. On our island home in Canada, *Camassia quamash* 'Azurea' ran down to the seaside, a synthesis of the gray-blue of the Pacific, the blue-black edging of the Coast Range Mountains and the overhanging amethyst sky — no wonder we thirst for a piece of it.

Seasonal progression

SPRING There are so many blue-flowered bulbs in spring you can almost taste them in the air: *Chionodoxa luciliae* looking up and *Scilla siberica* looking down, *Muscari armeniacum* scattered beneath *Stachyurus praecox* as if it has fallen from the shrub and turned blue. These pale blue dots show up well in the wan light. *Lathyrus vernus*, one of the most spectacular early blue herbaceous plants, gives an overwhelming, long-lasting display of clusters of miniature blue pea flowers fading to a beautiful Parma gray. *Vinca difformis*, a great performer, starts in February and carries its powder-blue flowers well into the following winter.

LATE SPRING By the end of May the gardener is spoiled from the choice of blue flowers. *Veronica gentianoides*, with its mat of shiny leaves, sends up spires of clear blue. The Dutch iris 'Ideal' is a perfect match for *Aquilegia flabellata*, and carries an ideal contrast in its chrome-yellow crest. *Philadelphus coronarius* 'Aureus' keeps its spring-green foliage into summer, setting off the moodier blues of *Scilla* (*Hyacinthoides*) *nonscripta*.

Powder blue *Camassia cusickii* is a seldom seen but easily grown bulb for heavy clay or damp earth. On the wall is one of the fastest growing *Ceanothus, C. arboreus* 'Trewithen Blue', which will make a fine small tree of 12–15 feet in as little as three years.

EARLY SUMMER The full size and exquisite pale color of *Iris germanica* 'Blue Sapphire' has every visitor asking for it. Is it their improbable, sculptural shape and ephemeral substance that leads us into an almost fetishlike collecting of iris. *Lupinus podophyllus* can just be seen coming into its second gray-blue flowering, having had the first flowers cut away as they faded. Seeded through the bed and blurring the edges are selections of *Aquilegia vulgaris. Phlox divaricata* 'Dirigo Ice' is long-flowering and low, sprawling over the boundary and rooting as it goes, quite like a strawberry. One of the choicest of this choice group belongs to a subspecies, *laphamii* — the brilliantly named 'Chattahoochee', which you must have, even if you can't pronounce it.

AUTUMN The autumnal blues are the most powerfully somber. *Agapanthus* 'Midnight Blue', with condensed inky blue clusters, is overhung by the much larger hybrid *Agapanthus* 'Hadspen' with paler, drooping flowers. *Campanula* must be the backbone of a blue planting throughout the season, and here *Campanula barbata* flaunts its milky, hairy blue bells in a second flowering. The strongest rhythm of this time is held by the great drumsticks of *Echinops bannaticus* 'Taplow Blue'. Throughout the area, replacing the *Aquilegia* of spring, *Nigella damascena* 'Miss Jekyll' has self-seeded so vigorously that it seems never to be out of flower. Our favorite *Clematis, C. viticella* is a late and robust bloomer, like 'Prince Charles', shown here. Pruned to the ground in the winter, it doesn't interfere with its hosts in the spring. *Salvia* does its best for the late show, of course; *Salvia patens* pulls out every stop to electrifying effect. The blue star of our year is *Cerinthe major* 'Purpurascens' with its intense glaucous leaves and purple-blue flowers — equally fantastic in pots or in the ground.

SPRING

SUMMER

AUTUMN

from top to bottom

PHLOX DIVARICATA 'DIRIGO ICE'

BORAGO LAXIFLORA

CARYOPTERIS X CLANDONENSIS 'HEAVENLY BLUE'

VERONICA GENTIANOIDES

NIGELLA DAMASCENA 'MISS JEKYLL'

LOBELIA SIPHILITICA

CENTAUREA MONTANA

ECHINOPS BANNATICUS 'TAPLOW BLUE'

GERANIUM WALLICHIANUM 'BUXTON'S VARIETY'

CAMASSIA LEICHTLINII CAERULEA GROUP

SCILLA PERUVIANA

CLEMATIS HERACLEIFOLIA 'WYEVALE'

LATHYRUS VERNUS CYANEUS

DELPHINIUM GRANDIFLORUM

CERATOSTIGMA WILLMOTTIANUM

MUSCARI ARMENIACUM

SALVIA PATENS

ACONITUM 'NEWRY BLUE'

GREEN is the

— sappy green fields, the green air of a woodland glen — everyone can revel in it. It is, of course, this thin layer of green plant cells that keeps us breathing, keeps us fed, keeps us alive. No wonder we adore it, long for it when without it. The changing seasons add the melody to the green of a planting. Spring shoots are often tinged with chartreuse, turn blue-green in their fullness, and fade to biscuit yellow in the autumn before they fall. The eye translates the fresh green of spring to excitement, change and newness, while the other side of this leafy coin is the melancholy of autumnal ambers and golds. Mood changes in a planting can be orchestrated with a twist of the color dial.

Surely green is the color of Pan, god of Life. Kirlian photography, which makes the invisible emanations of the psyche visible, concurs: green is the lush, sympathetic color. An all-green garden is very chic and, like any monochrome planting, can explore to a greater depth the nuances of tone, texture and rhythm. The choice is limitless, and this very abundance can make for difficulties. Unlike any other color, green is found on all levels, from ground-hugging mosses through herbaceous plants and shrubs to the tallest trees. It is all around, so omnipotent that it is no longer recognized as a color in its own right. One day when I was working in our long, double hosta border, surrounded by its golds, emeralds and dusty grays, a garden visitor remarked: "I am glad they are having you do some planting. It needs a little color." (I was planting *Nicotiana langsdorffii*, the green tobacco plant.) She could not see the color she was knee deep in.

Colors are rarely seen in isolation, so it is important always to be aware of the optical effect adjacent colors have on each other. Both Goethe in his theories of color harmony and Chevreul in his 700-page monograph of 1839 about the Gobelins dyers pointed out

color of primeval wealth

the phenomenon of successive contrast, the way in which the eye, staring first at a color and then at a piece of white paper, will see on the paper an afterimage in a complementary color. If the eye is fixed on green, the successive contrast will be red; if fixed on yellow, violet; if fixed on blue, orange — each shadow in perfect contrast. Seurat and Monet made use of this effect in creating the terrible depths of their canvases, and it results in a dazzling shimmer between pure red flowers and green leaves.

Being all-pervasive, green is the constant foil for other garden colors. The yellow borders at Hadspen are principally green; the blue border and the orange border are also green. Almost always, green provides the backdrop. It is the way color is played off against this green that will determine the success of a planting, and the attention paid to details like the exact tone of green and the shape of leaves in relation to the color of the flowers that will make of it a coherent piece of music. Mastery of this particular skill is exemplified in the large prairie-like plantings of the Dutch garden designer Piet Oudolf, and in the works of art based on subtle changes in the hue and texture of grasses created by the American-based designers Wolfgang Oehme and James van Sweden. A short, evenly clipped area of grass cuts through an intermediate rough stretch of grass, which, in turn, leads to swathes of long, exotic reeds — a monochrome in green. The textures are similar but build into a sublime and visually consuming image.

Understanding the use of green is essential in garden design. Unless it is mastered, all else will collapse. No feeling of strength or of continuity between the varying scales will be achieved unless this color is controlled, from the lowliest moss to the largest tree.

THE DISSECTED LEAVES OF *SAMBUCUS RACEMOSA* 'SUTHERLAND GOLD' FORM A HARMONIZING BACKDROP FOR *CAREX ELATA* 'BOWLES' GOLDEN', WHICH, WITH THE FRONDS OF PALE GREEN FENNEL (*FOENICULUM VULGARE*), MAKES A TEXTURAL CONTRAST WITH *HOSTA* 'BUCKSHAW BLUE'. SOMEWHAT LESS RAMPANT THAN THE COMMON PERIWINKLE, *VINCA MAJOR* 'MACULATA' SHARES ALL THESE GREENS AND TIES THE PICTURE TOGETHER.

Using green

Gardening reflects the social ethics of its period. The Georgians and Victorians liked to control nature and display their wealth, and well-clipped hedges and topiary met both objectives: yet today's electric trimmers bring these within everyone's reach. Are they now too achievable? Pursued as an end in themselves, they become a dead end. Geometric greenery is anyway a contradiction in terms — nature thwarted — but it appeals to our sense of *noir*. A flat green background can be used theatrically, to show off other colors and patterns: little else makes as good a backdrop to the many uprights of a perennial border as a fine boxwood or yew hedge. Ignore the myth that these are slow-growing; up to 3 feet a year can be expected if a hedge is properly planted. This means perfect drainage — a gravel run or drainage tiles in a 1 by 3 foot trench of farmyard muck, clean topsoil, and plenty of water provided through a dripline or by overhead irrigation. Sometimes there really is a right way to do things: do not even consider cutting corners or stinting on this particular aspect of planting. A hedge is a considerable feature in a garden, and a moth-eaten example will haunt you year-round. You can move a perennial, a shrub, even a tree; but moving a hedge that is not thriving is a major undertaking.

Gardening is an act of born-again nature worship, where we are all ready to bend our knees to the fickle, frosty diva. The year begins with plain green or buff plant lists and catalogs, their orthodox Latin texts (*Abeliophyllum*, *Abies*, *Abrotanella*, etc.) instilling an illusion of order. The après-winter look of the garden is reassuringly simple and minimalist, the few green shoots of *Leucojum* push through a promise of what is to come. This year we *will* keep up and comprehend it all.

Green is a secondary color, a mixture of the primary colors blue and yellow: one or the other usually predominates, and whether a leaf is blue-green or yellow-green can change the whole atmosphere of a planting. A shadow can be cast with a thick mass of gray-green *Hosta* 'Halcyon', an even darker one with the black-green strap leaves of *Ophiopogon planiscapus* 'Nigrescens'. An effective green planting is always

left THE LEVIATHAN *GUNNERA MANICATA* BEGINS TO UNFURL ITS GIANT GREEN BODY FAR TOO EARLY IN THE YEAR. LIKE A MALADJUSTED PET, IT IS WONDERFUL IN ITS CRANKY BEHAVIOR AND GRAND THORNY LEAVES. IT CANNOT BEAR TO HIBERNATE LONG ENOUGH, YET IS A MARTYR TO FROST. *DARMERA PELTATA* WITH ITS PARASOL LEAVES ENJOYS A DAMP POSITION, BUT WE HAVE GROWN IT IN SOME DRYISH SPOTS WHERE IT THRIVES AND ADDS A TROPICAL AMBIENCE.

right AMONG THE LUXURIANT RUGOSE LEAVES OF THE *RODGERSIA* PLANTINGS THE PLEATED LEAVES OF *VERATRUM VIRIDE* SEND UP A GREEN CANDELABRA OF FLOWERS IN FRONT OF THE SHUTTLECOCK FERN, *MATTEUCCIA STRUTHIOPTERIS.* THE TALL STRAP LEAVES BELONG TO *IRIS PSEUDACORUS,* WITH SMALLISH GREEN-YELLOW FLOWERS.

concerned with the use of darkness, and Édouard Vuillard's skillful manipulation of tone in his painting *Lunch at Vasony* is a lesson to all designers in the subtleties of this shadowy art.

Changes in texture are important. For a sense of the potential, consider the rugose leaves of *Rodgersia*, the glaucous matt blue-gray leaves of *Hosta* 'Hadspen Blue', and the shiny, almost silken leaves of *Hakonechloa macra* 'Alboaurea'. The differences between them may be straightforward, but a grouping of these three plants no more lacks complexity and interest than does a string trio: its very simplicity holds the key, and focuses attention on aspects of scale. Japanese moss gardens take this idea to its highest art: a small pine tree, a fern or a tuft of grass and some moss can be so arranged to form a mood-changing, visually captivating picture. Using such a limited palette is as challenging as playing a violin solo. Maintaining its interest depends on the skill with which the pattern — the melody of the piece — is repeated.

The green giant *Gunnera manicata* is all sinister, alien texture.

Thorny stems emerging from huge, hairy rhizomes carry equally the leaves up to 6 foot wide, which could shelter quite a party. In the autumn, *Gunnera* just curdles around the edges, when it is time to cut down the stems, tuck straw around next year's buds, and turn the leaves upside down over the rhizomes in a tented shape to shed the rain. Thus protected, these subtropical monsters will survive exceedingly cold weather. The biggest threat to them is late spring frosts, so leave this covering to be pushed aside by the new growth as it emerges.

Borrowed landscape is a great euphemism for all the other stuff visible from the garden — in our case, a perfect, pastoral, rolling, Somerset hill, with mature oaks and beeches on the ridge and hawthorn and blackthorn in the vale. It could as easily be a shopping mall or a car park; if it were, we would screen it out of the picture — but to be able to incorporate such splendid views into the garden is a huge gain. Green is the connecting tissue that binds the landscape to the garden and, even more, the garden to the landscape. Shrubs mimic the shapes of distant

... green is the connecting tissue that binds the landscape to the garden and the garden to the landscape ...

hummocky trees — remember that small-leaved trees will read as being farther away than large-leaved trees — and the eye links mounds of grass with distant grassy fields. Wind passing through *Miscanthus sinensis* or *Deschampsia cespitosa* entangles them visually with the cornfield beyond. It is important to plan out to the horizon, like Capability Brown, allowing no division or diversion to fall across the viewing line, no color but green, the ground-color of most plant life. Even the slightest color change can rivet the gaze, a single white foxglove slashing asunder that green connective tissue.

The savannah was the motherland of mankind, and perhaps this is why people have become preoccupied with lawns. In the days when even a small area of monocultured grasses was not obtainable, lawns had charm and visual interest. Some *Bellis perennis* were always at hand for a daisy chain. Now, with power mowers, rollers, rakes and edgers, and a chemical arsenal that would do any dictator proud, the ultimate has been achieved: a perfectly flat lawn of absolutely even surface, texture

and color, providing no visual stimulation whatsoever. The grail of the perfect lawn was not worth the quest — it is time to abandon it. A more natural, well-mottled lawn can tie the house to the landscape, issue an invitation to enter the garden, or provide the framework for a horticultural composition.

Greens, as all our mothers should have said, are good for us, but for too long has the soup been produced in an unadored and unadorned part of the garden. Yet nowhere else is there such opportunity to show off a display of green textures. No paints, silks or forests can compete with the variety offered by the leaves of the many forms of lettuce, while there are no finer glaucous leaves than those of a well-grown cabbage, none more fascinating than the deeply puckered green leaves of chard with their sensuous stems. The kitchen gardens of Villandry first showed the way to an understanding of the beauty of greens, but for more than twenty years, Joy Larkcom, the vegetable queen, has worshipped them in her gardening and her writing — *The*

Salad Garden, Creative Vegetable Gardening, The Vegetable Garden Displayed and more — and pursued the ideal to a high order of expertise.

It is intriguing how green flowers capture the imagination. Seed merchants fall over backwards to produce green zinnias, green *Amaranthus*, green *Nicotiana*; there is even a green rose, the curious *Rosa chinensis* 'Viridiflora'. Although these have all, with the exception of the rose, been specifically developed for their novelty value, they come into their own in a monochrome scheme. A conventional flower shape in an unexpected color, as in the zinnia 'Envy' or the snowdrop-like *Galtonia viridiflora*, is the hook that catches our attention. When the familiar is altered, even so slightly, it rings bells in the psyche, and so the green bells of Ireland, *Moluccella laevis*, are riveting. In a monochrome planting, an unexpected change of scale is a delight. The galingale, *Cyperus longus*, is 2 foot tall, its Egyptian cousin the giant reed, *C. papyrus*, six times that; both grasses have triangular stems and heads like firework explosions,

but the difference in size makes you want to examine them in detail. Such sensory surprises as these are all the more effective when they come singly, and need not be confined to color or to scale — consider the melted-honey scent of the greenish catkins of *Itea ilicifolia*, or the foul stink of the beautiful flower of *Cobaea scandens alba*, that remarkable climbing plant whose natural pollinator is a bat.

In a woodland setting, the improbable textures of Indian poke, *Veratrum viride*, from the damp forests of the Pacific coast, look other-worldly, unfolding smooth leaves pleated as precisely as a fan and uncurling a wirelike spike of green flowers. An outlandish partner for this plant would be a cluster of *Paris polyphylla*, with leaves like *Trillium* but a ruffle of green sepals and petals for a flower. Baby's tears or mind-your-own-business, *Soleirolia* (formerly *Helxine*) *soleirolii*, which looks like a moss but on close inspection is not, and *Selaginella kraussiana*, a perennial that has decided to mimic sphagnum moss, would both enjoy these same moist conditions, and make a spongy green carpet for this planting.

SPRING

SUMMER

AUTUMN

from top to bottom

TULIPA 'SPRING GREEN'

ANGELICA ARCHANGELICA

KNIPHOFIA 'PERCY'S PRIDE'

HELLEBORUS FOETIDUS

NICOTIANA ALATA 'LIME GREEN'

EUCOMIS COMOSA

ERYNGIUM GIGANTEUM

FRITILLARIA IMPERIALIS

PETROSELINUM CRISPUM

 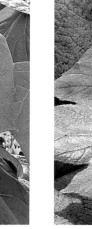  

HOSTA 'FRANCES WILLIAMS'
LACTUCA SATIVA 'COCARDE'
PAULOWNIA TOMENTOSA

BRUNNERA MACROPHYLLA 'HADSPEN CREAM'
CYNARA CARDUNCULUS SCOLYMUS GROUP
ASTILBOIDES TABULARIS

LUPINUS 'CHANDELIER'
FICUS CARICA 'BROWN TURKEY'
HOSTA 'FRANCEE'

YELLOW is

to Nirvana for the Buddhist; it is the golden halo of the saint. Man has always held it in high esteem: the Aztecs worshipped it, Dorothy followed it, we just love it. In yoga philosophy, where the chakras are the seven areas of the body that concentrate the life force, it is believed that yellow emanates from the solar plexus, the center of human self-recognition and self-worth. This yellow is more valuable than any gold sought by means of the philosopher's stone, though gold itself has always been imbued with magic properties.

Yellow is central in the spectrum of light visible to humans, bending through green to the cool of blue on one side, and through orange to the warmth of red on the other. It reflects more of the light that strikes it than does any other color, giving it a preternatural brightness. With its maximum reflectiveness and the fact that sunlight is mostly in the yellow range — the sun being seen as yellow — it is small wonder that so many flowers have evolved in this color. At Rudolf Steiner's Waldorf school, rooms painted yellow were used to focus the mental activity of twelve-year-olds. Monet used a particularly singing canary yellow in his dining room, understanding intuitively its creative powers. Like a beam of light, yellow can illuminate the darkest corner. A shadowy path can be dappled with the light of *Primula vulgaris*, while a yellow light in a hallway reads as sunlight. From Canadian prairies rippling with wheat or English fields of impossibly yellow mustard to the acres of sunflowers that inspired Van Gogh, yellow exudes the assurance of self-satisfied fullness, of harvest.

One of the observable facts that is not part of the contrivance of the standard color wheel is that when two colors of the same saturation are mixed together (for example, yellow and blue), the resulting color always absorbs more light than either of the original hues

the light at the entrance

and appears darker. When two colors of identical saturation are juxtaposed, a vibration or shimmering seems to occur — the rods in the eye, sensitive to light and dark but not to color, read each color as the same tone, while the cones, sensitive to color, register the differences between the two. Thus a conundrum is sent to the brain, and reality begins to wobble. Except in extreme cases, even the color-blind can see in the yellow range: related to green (unlike red, for example), yellow flowers do not form any complex clashes with their own leaves, so no retinal confusion strains the eye or interferes with the progress of the theme.

Lead or barium chromate, which gives its name to chrome yellow, provided the only pure yellow available to the artist until the twentieth century, but the yellowish earth colors of ochre and sienna have long been used — think of color-washed Italian buildings. The yellows nature so likes are formed by the various carotenoid pigments. These include both xanthophyll, responsible for the yellow in roses, and the see-in-the-dark Vitamin-A carotene of carrots, which also causes the red of boiled lobsters.

Yellow is simple — unlike red or blue, the other primary colors, it does not drift off the visible spectrum into the imperceptibilities of infrared or ultraviolet — yet its simplicity belies its power and range. It so dominates the color of our lives that we tend to lose awareness of it and control. The high chartreuse side of yellow looks like spring itself in the wan and watery light of an English spring, while the chrome yellows and copper yellows virtually define autumn. So automatically is the yellow of autumnal leaves associated with the beginning of winter that a planting or painting of this hue can easily trigger a state of melancholy.

WAVES OF *ANTHEMIS TINCTORIA*, A.T. 'E.C. BUXTON' AND *A.T.* 'KELWAYI' DESCEND THE SLOPE AND DEEPEN IN TONE AS THE FIRST TO HOLD SWAY IS SUCCEEDED BY THE NEXT. THE AMBER *RUDBECKIA HIRTA* 'IRISH EYES' WILL BECOME THE DOMINANT TONE AS THIS BORDER NEARS AUTUMN. THE PALE YELLOW SPIRES BELONG TO *LINARIA DALMATICA* — "A PLANT WITHOUT FAULT," SAYS GRAHAM STUART THOMAS. *L. DALMATICA*, WHICH SELF-SEEDS IF YOU ARE LUCKY, GROWS HERE WITH *POTENTILLA RECTA PALLIDA*.

Using yellow

In its origins, the herbaceous border is but an extension of the roadside shoulder, humbler people used to dig up shrubs and flowers from beside the road and plant them along their cottage paths. When Romanticism became fashionable early in the nineteenth century, its protagonists were not slow to notice how much prettier these borders were than the grand formal gardens of the rich, and set about emulating them. Needless to say, roadside natives were overlooked in favor of the exotic plants then beginning to be imported from around the world. It was not until the twentieth century that the arrangement of these borders came to be considered an art, and only recently has this form of gardening entered its colorist phase.

A monochrome planting can hold the tension, while mixed colors cancel each other out. A hodge-podge mixture of contrasting colors can be like what happens when a monkey runs up and down a piano keyboard. Possibly something meaningful is produced, but it is not likely. This sort of block planting — several of the same plant, isolated from their bedmates, making great slabs of unrelated color — is the antithesis of what we want to achieve. To weave all together, always planting so that one species overlaps and mingles with and lounges on the next incumbent, is our aim.

The sun always shines from a yellow planting. The simplicity of a monochrome design induces concentration on the finer details of texture, rhythm and syncopated contrast in planting, yet so many flowers have yellow petals, a yellow eye, yellow stamens. So many herbaceous plants, shrubs and trees have yellow leaves, stems or trunks that there is an enormous palette to work from. Often the color of a petal can be picked up in the eye of the next flower, and then in a leaf, to unify a grouping. An example of such a planting might be *Verbascum chaixii*, *Potentilla recta pallida* and *Aquilegia vulgaris* Vervaeneana Group.

The garden at Hadspen is planted in a series of movements, unified by a repeating theme running through the half-mile of borders. The excitement comes from experimenting with the principles of

LUPINUS 'CHANDELIER', OUR STANDARD
LIGHT IN THE YELLOW BORDER, IS
KEPT BLOOMING FOR A LONG TIME BY
DEADHEADING; IN LATE SPRING WE ALSO
PUT A YOUNG PLANT AT THE BASE OF
EVERY OLD ONE, TO FLOWER IN THE LATE
SUMMER. THE GRAY FERNLIKE FOLIAGE OF
ACHILLEA 'MOONSHINE' ENJOYS THE SAME
SUNNY SITE. AS THE ACHILLEA FADES,
ARGYRANTHEMUM 'JAMAICA PRIMROSE'
AND *TROPAEOLUM MAJUS* FILL IN AND
WILL CONTINUE UNTIL THE FROSTS.

organization while bending them to aesthetic use. The double yellow
borders, for example, we have planted like two tunes, related but
individual, too, twisted together visually. *Argyranthemums, Anthemis,
Thymophylla* and *Buphthalmum* are planted in repeated groupings, but
with ascending numbers of plants in each group along the left-hand
border, and descending numbers on the right; their yellow daisy-flowers
hold the contrapuntal melodies together. We use green fennel
(*Foeniculum vulgare*), a neutral green of unfocused texture, to back solid
shapes such as the absurd and frivolous parrot tulips, or any other plant
or group we want to highlight — in much the same way as a portrait
painter will sometimes throw the background of a picture out of focus
in order to concentrate attention on the subject. Further subtlety is
achieved by planting pale yellow tulips on the uphill side of the repeating
fennel clumps, and varieties in a deeper yellow on the downhill side.
Walk down between the borders, turn around and look uphill — the
color of the composition deepens by a whole tone.

... yellow flowers do not form any complex clashes with their own leaves ...

Tall plantings of slender see-through plants such as *Linaria dalmatica* and *Digitalis lutea* allow voyeuristic glimpses of solid-colored subjects to the rear and increase the three-dimensional quality of the border. The use of high planting to the front with shorter flashy subjects like tulips or lilies kept to the back also tends to produce a feeling of intimacy and secret understanding.

All this yellow and green saturates the eye; the mind overflows with these closely related colors, and seeks an alternative. Tiny dots of blue will rest the eye — we use *Brunnera macrophylla* in spring and *Geranium pratense* later — and enable it to perceive even more yellow. After all, our intention with these borders is to turn up the volume: we want to take the yellow experience right off the scale.

The critical factor in all planting is of course light. The dramatic effect of moving from light to shadow never loses its impact. As you move from sunshine to shade, the warmth on your cheek turns to a chill.

left FRAGRANT *SPARTIUM JUNCEUM*, HAVING BEEN CUT BACK IN MARCH, WILL PROVIDE AN ABUNDANCE OF PEA-FLOWERS FOR MONTHS, AND THERE IS MORE FRAGRANCE FROM WARM YELLOW *ROSA* 'GRAHAM THOMAS', THE BEST OF DAVID AUSTIN'S ENGLISH ROSES. LONG SPIKES OF TINY YELLOW *DIGITALIS LUTEA* RISE UP THROUGH *CALENDULA* 'PACIFIC APRICOT'.

right PALE YELLOW PETALS OF THE PERFECTLY NAMED ROSE 'GOLDEN WINGS' ARE MIMICKED BY THOSE OF *POTENTILLA RECTA PALLIDA*, ONE OF THE MANY INVALUABLE HERBACEOUS POTENTILLAS. THE FAMILY RESEMBLANCE EXTENDS FROM THEIR SILKY PETALS TO THEIR VELVETY STAMENS, AND THEY SEEM TO ENJOY BEING ENTANGLED WITH ONE ANOTHER. GIVEN PERSISTENT DEADHEADING, THEY WILL PERFORM TOGETHER THROUGHOUT THE SEASON.

Colors change as abruptly — a rose that looks bleached yellow in sunshine becomes a warm golden glow in shadow. The pupils of the eyes, pinpoints in sun, open in lowered light; colors rush in and saturate the retina; the senses revel in them.

From shadow toward light is the big effect, the feeling of elation, as when the sun comes over the horizon or the spotlight picks out the prima donna; but the angle of the light and the time of day that sunlight strikes a planting are vital, too. It makes so much difference to the perception of color whether a planting is backlit, sun streaming through petals as through a stained-glass window, or has the sun full upon it: a flat lighting is good for saturated pigments. The deeper chrome yellows of sunflowers and rudbeckias show off to best advantage in such full-frontal light, as inspection of Van Gogh's sunflower paintings will show. A poppy, a peony and a primrose, with tissue-paper petals, become flames in the wind with light behind them. Our yellow borders are planted running east-west, and the cool morning sun backlights the

viewing line from the top of the path. Particularly in summer, noonday sun does such hideous things to the way the eye sees color, deadening and draining it, that the garden is then best left to the mad dogs until afternoon, when it can be enjoyed again in long shadows and amber light.

The many yellow and yellow-variegated foliage plants available are used to weave a strong background on which to work the theme of our picture. The filigreed foliage of *Sambucus racemosa* 'Sutherland Gold' gives good background height to a planting of *Lupinus* 'Chandelier' with hybrid *Kniphofia* 'Hadspen' and *Hosta* 'Hadspen Samphire' and 'Sum and Substance', with a spray of *Carex elata* 'Aurea' to carry the eye to the path edge. In temperate climates many valuable herbaceous plants such as lupins will bloom throughout the season if they are deadheaded regularly. As soon as a few of the lower flowers have faded, be brave and cut back the stalk. You will be rewarded in a few days with, usually, two or three spikes to replace the one. Even midsummer *Anthemis* will take an encore with the rudbeckias if they are shorn after their first

left CITRONELLA GROUP LILIES PUSH UP BETWEEN *CORTADERIA SELLOANA* 'AUREOLINEATA' AND A PLANTING OF *TANACETUM NIVEUM*, REPLACING *TULIPA* 'YOKOHAMA', AND *BUPHTHALMUM SALICIFOLIUM* IS WAITING TO FILL THE SATURATED YELLOW SLOT. THIS DROUGHT-TOLERANT *TANACETUM* HAS BECOME ONE OF OUR MUST-HAVE PLANTS, ITS YELLOW EYE FITTING IT INTO THIS ENSEMBLE. WITH ATTRACTIVE GRAY-GREEN LEAVES, IT WILL TIRELESSLY SEND UP SPRAYS OF LITTLE DAISIES LIKE THESE ALL SUMMER.

right *TULIPA* 'FIRST LADY', ON THE LEFT, AND *T.* 'GREUZE', ON THE RIGHT, PICK OUT THE COLORS OF THE BLEEDING HEARTS ON *DICENTRA SPECTABILIS* 'GOLDHEART', WHOSE ABSOLUTE DISCORD OF LEAF AND FLOWER WOULD PLEASE ANY KEITH JARRETT JAZZ FAN. SUCH PERFECTLY CONTRADICTORY HUES AS THOSE OF OUR NEW *DICENTRA* ARE NOT VERY COMMONLY FOUND ON A SINGLE PLANT, BUT OCCUR MORE FREQUENTLY THAN MIGHT BE SUPPOSED.

flush. With a plant that is just the right color, it is often a good tactic to have a lot where you want it. Cut back a third of the buds before they flower to delay them, and let a third linger on past their flowering peak, thus ensuring a very long impact period. This treatment can be excellent with *Solidago*, even with *Aster* and *Achillea*.

There are few objects in this world that have more romance than a rose in full bloom, but many are difficult to use in a monochrome planting. Not only may the petals fade or, in the case of China roses, deepen in color as they age, but the color may change more obviously; several yellow roses blush pink as they develop, and many begin with an orange flash and then become a peach tending toward pink as they fade. Many of the modern shrub roses meet our criteria of health, structure and length of flowering, but 'Graham Thomas' is particularly good, as fine and long lasting as its namesake. Only the pale yellow butterflies of 'Golden Wings' can hold a candle to this comparative newcomer, although we have found the climber 'Leverkusen', with its

glossy leaves similar to those of *Rosa wichuriana*, to be very successful with its young trails bent over long bamboo canes to form a flowering latticework, through which we grow *Eremurus stenophyllus*, unstaked.

The appeal of the cottage garden is its relaxed charm: as William Robinson wrote in *The English Flower Garden*, "It is the absence of any pretentious pattern which lets the flowers tell their story to the heart." The self-set seedlings of *Oenothera biennis* and *O. stricta, Aquilegia chrysantha* and *A. longissima* fall between the wandering shoots of *Solidago* and *Anthemis*, all adding to the natural, intricate effect. This type of planting can be seen taken to a brilliant conclusion in the garden of Ton ter Linden at Ruines in Holland, and is probably most easily understood from the photographs of Marijke Heuff. Tight control of the theme combined with a loose hand in the creative weeding makes this style the jazz of gardening. Yellow is a simple color to use, as uncomplicated as a tin whistle. The brightness of the melody holds the power in this planting, many uprights carrying the rhythm forward.

Seasonal progression

SPRING The watery light of spring casts a pale yellow-enhancing haze over the landscape. With so much new growth showing chartreuse — new shoots on *Pterocarya fraxinifolia*, the unfurling leaves of the beech hedge, even grasses like *Carex elata* 'Aurea' — *Primula veris* can only harmonize. The pure yellow of 'West Point' tulips is needed to carry the color forward from the narcissus blooms they replace. Among *Euphorbia* species, there are many of great garden value, from the deciduous *E. polychroma* and its taller cousin *E. palustris* to the evergreen *E. nicaeensis* and procumbent *E. myrsinites*. Here *E. characias* can be counted on for a long spring show, its tall black-eyed clusters of yellowish bracts lending structure and matching the new shoots of the heavily pollarded *Sambucus racemosa* 'Sutherland Gold'. After the last frost, our favorite grass, *Hakonechloa macra* 'Alboaurea', emerges like yellow silk from its tuft of roots. Clumped *Leucojum aestivum* 'Gravetye Giant' are slow to develop their long-lasting blooms, which look like giant snowdrops. In spring the promise is the thing: every bud is a note yet to be played.

SUMMER The full-frontal light of summer sun enhances clear yellows. Ubiquitous it may be, but *Alchemilla mollis* is not to be ignored. When it becomes dowdy it can be cut right back, to rejuvenate within a few days. Its yellow sprays make the transition from green to the higher purity of yellow in *Lupinus* 'Chandelier'. In 'Golden Wings', the ideal single-flowered shrub rose, even its ornament of stamens is in tune. The pert uprightness of *Sisyrinchium striatum* has an almost comical air. With its copper-tipped leaves, *Hypericum androsaemum* is one of the most useful of its species for treatment as a herbaceous plant; the yellow flowers are a bonus. Year after year, wispy *Digitalis lutea* will produce its tiny foxgloves for months if judiciously deadheaded. Green fennel is used here in a supporting role, to cover the bare legs of *Sambucus racemosa* 'Sutherland Gold' and to add to the lovely froth of the golden Manchurian weed *Sisymbrium luteum. Cephalaria gigantea*, like a tall *Scabiosa*, hovers behind the rose 'Golden Wings'. Beneath these summer flowers, the autumnal-colored leaves are gaining strength, awaiting their turn in the sun.

AUTUMN In autumn the more saturated yellows look good in low-angled sunlight. Daisies dominate. *Dyssodia tenuiloba* (syn. *Thymophylla tenuiloba*) is a fragrant native of Texas, which we picked up on the roadside in South Africa, and another pantropical weed, *Bidens bipinnata*, weaves dark-eyed dots of chrome-yellow flowers up through the closely allied *Coreopsis lanceolata*. No autumnal scene is complete without the *Rudbeckia hirta* 'Irish Eyes' (often wrongly listed as an annual but in its third year here); *R. fulgida* var. *sullivantii* 'Goldsturm', the dark center making it yet another black-eyed-susan; and *R. maxima*, destined to be tall. By the feet of *Oenothera biennis*, the diminutive and demure *Solidago* 'Goldenmosa' is one representative of this huge and thuggish family with restrained good manners; *Solidago canadensis* flowers later and works in well with the vigorous yet graceful spires of *Epilobium angustifolium album*, which spreads but does not seed. These robustly colonizing plants terrify gardeners, but need not. Planted together, they push each other around in an energetic balancing act.

SPRING

SUMMER

AUTUMN

from top to bottom

EUPHORBIA POLYCHROMA

POTENTILLA RECTA PALLIDA

OENOTHERA BIENNIS

PRIMULA VULGARIS 'VAL HORNCASTLE'

CEPHALARIA GIGANTEA

HELIANTHUS ANNUUS

DICENTRA SPECTABILIS 'GOLDHEART'

ALLIUM FLAVUM

BETA VULGARIS 'GOLDEN CHARD'

FRITILLARIA IMPERIALIS 'MAXIMA LUTEA'

ANTHEMIS TINCTORIA 'E.C. BUXTON'

HELENIUM 'BUTTERPAT'

DORONICUM ORIENTALE 'MAGNIFICUM'

ACHILLEA FILIPENDULINA 'GOLD PLATE'

RUDBECKIA HIRTA 'IRISH EYES'

TULIPA 'YOKOHAMA'

PHLOMIS LONGIFOLIA

ROSA 'GRAHAM THOMAS'

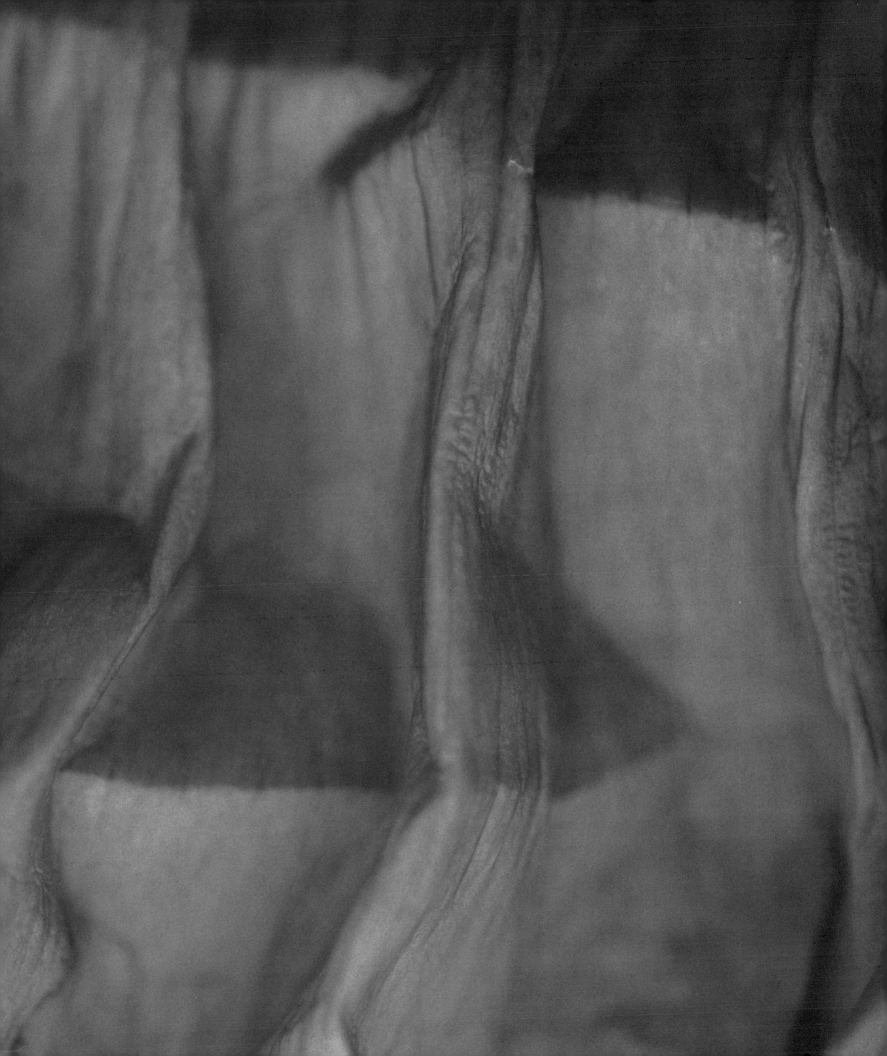

ORANGE is

and paprika are its essence — and like spice, it slowly warms, invigorates, and imparts a gentle strength. From the hot side of the color wheel, a zesty combination of red's vitality and yellow's light, orange is bold and will always sing out from any planting. No matter what angle it is approached from, it will be obvious and assertive. It is also a color with staying power. Natural tones of orange never become tiresome to look at or lose their interest — nor can orange ever be accused of withdrawing into the background.

Probably the most misunderstood and unappreciated color, orange has lately become unfashionable in some gardening circles — little wonder, perhaps, in the face of constant visual assault by rude combinations in garish public plantings, and in the endless new harshly toned floribunda and hybrid tea roses, which have misleadingly been described as "eye-catching vermilion" or "vivid coral." Only a Frankenstein-inspired breeding program could produce such synthetic representations of this pure-spirited color.

"Oh, I could not possibly have orange in the garden!" a visitor once exclaimed, as though referring to a noxious pest or disease. Yet orange is not a color to be dismissed or banished, rather one with which to celebrate and exult, the color of joy. Its glowing tones and shades in a color scheme can bring to mind vivid images and impressions — Mediterranean terraces, African landscapes, a dramatic sunrise, a basket of tangy Seville oranges. Saffron, the shade particularly associated with Buddhist monks, is not shrieking but transcendental, and the shades of terra-cotta, sienna and umber based on earth pigments have been used through history, worldwide. Each culture since the beginning of time has developed its own method of extracting these pigments for decorating bodies, crockery and textiles.

spice — cinnamon, turmeric

Color is known to be therapeutic. Chromotherapy, the tradition of healing through the use of colored minerals, crystals and ointments, dyes and colored chambers, dates back thousands of years to the Egyptians, Chinese and Indians. In such treatments, orange is held to energize certain organs and areas of the body and is recommended if you feel lethargic or depressed, or are inhibited. Color energies are said to be absorbed through the skin and the wearing of colored clothing; silk is thought to be the finest material for this transmission, bringing to mind images of the Dalai Lama, yogis, and enlightened multitudes in colorful silk saris. A study of the psychological effects of color in interior design by Henner Ertel found that an orange environment caused children to be more cheerful and sociable, less irritable and hostile. It also revealed the positive effect of color on the intellect, showing that children's IQ scores rose by up to twelve points in an orange setting. Clearly an orange planting could provide the ultimate therapy for both mind and body.

The flora of South Africa's Cape region is the richest in the world, and unusual in the range of genera that it encompasses that are found there and nowhere else. It is to be seen at its best in the *fynbos*, Afrikaans for *fine bush*, an area composed mostly of heath vegetation. A visit to this part of the Cape in October would surely serve to sweep away any lingering remnants of prejudice against orange. Stunning displays of proteas offer every shade of orange in exotic flowers the shape of large sea anemones surrounded by papery bracts of the same color. Rushlike reeds, *Platycaulos compressus*, flower with plumes of rust, and *Watsonia*, the bugle lilies, emerge as flaming spires. While the heathers, such as *Erica* 'Coccinea', *E. mammosa* and *E.* 'Grandiflora,' are more vivid than you ever dreamed possible.

Using orange

Orange, by nature stimulating and exciting, displays these qualities nowhere better than in the garden. If you are hungry for these sensations — and most gardeners are — use orange to satiate your appetite. Lace your borders with the piquant flavors of tangerine, marmalade and ginger offered from spring bulbs, summer perennials and autumn annuals. Orange calls forth other responses, too. Everyone likes to sit by a fire, not just for the heat but for the sheer pleasure of the crackling, sizzling orange flames; and the blazing orange of a sunset can take your breath away. The same exhilaration will be generated by an orange planting scheme in the garden — it will be warming and elating.

At Hadspen we follow the imperative of orange from spring to autumn, indulging ourselves totally in a monochrome border planted with herbaceous plants, shrubs and climbers. Working with a single color is a challenge requiring the implementation of many design techniques to bring all the shades and tones together in a unified theme. One way of doing this is to use a single genus in different shades, and herbaceous

Potentilla works particularly well in an orange scheme. *Potentilla* x *tonguei*, apricot with a red center; *P.* 'William Rollison', double orange with a yellow reverse to the petals; and *P.* 'Gloire de Nancy', velvety double scarlet with an orange reverse scramble and weave through the border, animating the whole.

The daylilies also offer many selections in this color range, with yellow-orange *Hemerocallis middendorffii*, tawny *H. fulva*, and rich terracotta-scarlet *H.* 'Aztec'. In a scheme planted in this way it is easy to follow the repeated patterns as they thread along the border, and to appreciate their tonal qualities. Monochrome plantings enable the eye to focus on individual details and on the intricacies of the design, and since eye and brain are not struggling with ever-changing color, as in a mixed planting, the experience will be refreshing rather than distracting.

Around the South Cottage at Sissinghurst Castle in Kent, England, Vita Sackville-West created the Sunset Garden, a combination of yellow, orange and red — great bold clumps of *Achillea* creeping happily

alongside *Solidago*, punctuated by *Kniphofia* and *Canna*. The cottage, its ancient brick walls a perfect backdrop for a planting such as this, contained the bedrooms, so each day began and ended with a walk through the garden. As Jane Brown wrote in *Sissinghurst: Portrait of a Garden*, "Hence the garden of the South Cottage fitted this pattern — it was to be there, cheerfully waiting for its occupants to greet the morning, and it was there, ready again, glowing in the early evening; in the morning the rising sun splashed the Irish yews, and in the evening setting sun gave the sunset colors of Vita's flowers a wonderful glow."

The same colors and indeed some of the same plants are used in a totally different way by Wendy and Michael Perry at Bosvigo House in Cornwall, England. They have chosen a semishaded woodland corner in which to display a wonderfully brazen composition styled with discerning talent and skill: a perfect balance of orange enhanced by chrome yellows and somber dark foliage makes this planting glow out of the shade. Shape and form are treated with the same impeccable attention — upright spires opposed by mounds, polished leaves contrasted with frothy foliage — to draw the eye the length and breadth of this abundant, almost junglelike planting and ensure that every plant and combination receives the attention it deserves.

Stone, timber and brick, the natural building materials of garden architecture, all lend themselves to sympathetic and complementary associations with orange. Try a tangle of *Lonicera* x *tellmanniana* mixed with the amber of *Rosa* 'Easlea's Golden Rambler' against an old brick wall; *Eschscholzia californica* or *Helianthemum* 'Henfield Brilliant' alongside brick paving, or a terracotta pot planted with *Arctotis* x *hybrida* 'Flame' or the *Dahlia* 'Ellen Houston'. The textures involved are all organic, whether living or inert: combining them highlights the subtle tonal changes in each to enhance the whole.

When designing a planting, whatever the color, it must be remembered that foliage — green, gray or silver, brown, plum, or bronze — will actually predominate. It is therefore important that flower

. . . orange is not a color to be dismissed or banished, rather one with which to celebrate and exult . . .

plantings should be big and bold, to ensure that the intensity of the color of the blooms is not diffused by that of the leaves. Leaf and flower color must also be considered from another point of view: how do they set one another off? Brown and bronze foliages in particular come to life when combined with orange, but all foliage is enhanced by its vibrancy. Associations of orange with dark green, lime green, silvery gray and deep plum all make appealing groupings — a zingy combination of orange and deep plum in the same plant is to be found in *Ligularia dentata* 'Desdemona' and *Berberis* x *ottawensis*. Bronze *Foeniculum vulgare* 'Purpureum' (fennel) is our desert island plant, the plant we would not want to be without. Invaluable in the spring as emerging hazy foliage that combines with orange tulips — 'Orange Favorite' or 'Golden Artist,' it is cut back in the summer to encourage new growth. Finally in later summer, as it flowers, we strip off its old leaves to expose bamboolike stems. These stems and the seedheads make excellent architectural subjects when edged with late autumn frosts.

ALTHOUGH PERFECTLY ROBUST, THE
SHRUB *COLUTEA X MEDIA* ASSUMES AN
ETHEREAL QUALITY AT THE BACK OF
THE BORDER, ITS DELICATE LEGUMINOUS
COPPER-ORANGE FLOWERS DANGLING
AMID THE SMALL SAGE-GREEN LEAVES.
LILIUM 'FIRE KING' PROVIDES A STRONG
CONTRAST IN FLOWER AND LEAF SHAPE,
WHILE ITS BOLD DARK UMBER BLOOMS
PICK UP THE ORANGE FLECKS IN THE
FLOWERS OF *COLUTEA*.

Many of the perennials that might be chosen for use in an orange planting make towering or robust clumps capable of providing much of the structure and substance essential to every border. *Lychnis chalcedonica* offers numerous flat heads of vibrant orange over a long period in early summer, and if the spent blooms are cut back by 2 to 3 inches to where new growth can be seen on the stems, it will flower again in August. Plan an orange border in your garden if only to pay homage to those Goliaths, the red-hot pokers (*Kniphofia* species and their hybrids), and contrast their fiery spikes with the large daisyshape flowers in shades of yellow, orange and brown belonging to *Helenium* or *Gazania* species. Orange also demands the presence of *Crocosmia*; thanks to more than a century of breeding, they offer a fine selection to add to the list of orange performers: 'Star of the East' with large blooms; 'Emily McKenzie' in dark orange with red streaks; and deep apricot 'Solfaterre'; which has the added bonus of brownish foliage. All *Crocosmia* foliage is a great asset to the border with its impressive tufts of swordlike green

left COMICALLY FURRY BUDS AND FAT SEEDPODS BELIE THE HIGH-VOLTAGE IMPACT OF THIS CLUMP OF *PAPAVER ORIENTALE* 'SAFFRON'. IT LOOKS ALMOST TOO POWERFUL TO TOUCH. A VELVETY BROWN *IRIS GERMANICA* PROVIDES DARK SHADOW BEHIND THE POPPIES WHILE THE FLOWERS OF *HELIANTHEMUM* 'HENFIELD BRILLIANT', ON THE PATH EDGE, CATCH THE LAST RAYS OF SUNLIGHT.

right A FLOCK OF PARROT TULIPS 'ORANGE FAVORITE' IS SET OFF BY THE FINE YOUNG COPPER FOLIAGE OF *FOENICULUM VULGARE* 'PURPUREUM' (BRONZE FENNEL). ITS HAZY LEAVES THROW THE BACKGROUND OUT OF FOCUS. THE VIBRANT LEAVES OF *HEMEROCALLIS* PICK UP THE APPLE-GREEN FEATHERINGS ON THE PETALS OF THE TULIPS.

leaves — wonderfully pleated in 'Lucifer' — which remain unscathed by pest or disease from the moment they emerge in early spring until their last tan-colored remnants are cleared away in winter.

The time has come for gardeners to be more adventurous in their use of annuals. Two orange ones that certainly deserve more attention are *Leonotis nepetifolia*, with whorls of fuzzy orange flowers like a bergamot gone wrong, and the evening primrose *Oenothera versicolor* 'Sunset Boulevard'. At Hadspen we also enjoy using some of our earliest favorite plants for this color scheme. The thrill of growing a sunflower never dies, and with the new varieties available, it is even more exciting. Try planting *Helianthus annuus* 'Velvet Queen' in rich mahogany — a dark saturation of orange — or 'Sunburst', with zonal shadings of yellow, apricot and orange. All will make an impressive statement.

Many people turn up their noses at marigolds and nasturtiums, but there is no room for plant snobbery or exclusiveness in our garden. Besides, when the rusts, coppers and chromes of the French or African

marigolds (*Tagetes* species) are placed next to brunette fennel or fawn *Carex*, they are hardly recognizable as the same plants that provide a shrieking spectacle in city park beds. In our orange border, nasturtiums (*Tropaeolum majus*) in a mixture of deep yellow, hot orange and scarlet race through and around other plants and up the wall; their more refined perennial cousin, *Tropaeolum tuberosum* var. *lineamaculatum* 'Ken Aslet', has small trumpets of orange with yellow throats and makes an interesting addition.

Orange speaks, ultimately, of autumn days, of great pumpkins and squashes, of tawny leaves and amber flowers. The whole countryside turns itself orange. Do these colors know how superbly they will be set off by the long, low rays of autumn light? We take pleasure in these signs of seasonal change, but not because we long for the lazy days of summer to be gone. We are spellbound and misled by the sheer glory of this autumnal bliss, tricked into forgetting that the icy fingers of winter will soon beckon us to the orange flames of the fireside.

Seasonal progression

SPRING The season for orange begins very slowly and delicately, as though nature realizes we need to accustom ourselves gradually to its blazing presence after the months of hibernation. Spears of *Euphorbia griffithii* 'Fireglow', looking as delicious and tempting as the early shoots of asparagus, give us the first glimpses; as the *Euphorbia* grows, its foliage is the perfect accompaniment to the streaked orange blooms of the tulip 'Golden Artist'. The smaller species tulip, *Tulipa praestans* 'Fusilier', is one of the earliest to come into bloom, its bright orange-scarlet flowers shrilling like sirens to announce the first days of spring. *Fritillaria imperialis* 'The Premier', complete with fancy headdress, oversees the spring parade from the back of the border. Place these *Fritillaria* where their unsightly dying foliage will be screened by the emerging leaves of neighboring herbaceous plants. Handmade supports of green bamboo hoops (*Sasa palmata*) are in place ready for the burgeoning of taller perennials, while the swordlike leaves of *Crocosmia* and smooth foliage of *Papaver somniferum* in varying shades of green provide a fresh backdrop.

SUMMER The gray pinnate-leaved shrub *Colutea × media*, with its burnt-orange pealike flowers, the scarlet crosiers of *Crocosmia* 'Lucifer' and the towering annual *Leonotis nepetifolia* combine to provide summer's background. Fuzzy foliage of bronze fennel (*Foeniculum vulgare* 'Purpureum') makes a netlike support for the intertwining, scrambling stems of the double herbaceous *Potentilla* 'William Rollison'. This bicolor flower of scarlet with a yellow reverse makes it a perfect plant to use transitionally as the border moves from yellow to orange to scarlet. The tulips have been removed after flowering and their precious space used for *Arctotis × hybrida* 'Flame', a half-hardy South African daisy that will continue to flower until the first frost. The orange-tinged foliage of *Euphorbia griffithii* 'Fireglow' is now highlighted by the deep orange-scarlet blooms of *Hemerocallis* 'Aztec Furnace' and the annual *Oenothera versicolor* 'Sunset Boulevard'. Backlit *Crocosmia* leaves and the chartreuse foliage of a feverfew, *Tanacetum parthenium* 'Aureum', provide a sharp contrast to the paler greens.

AUTUMN *Helianthus annuus* 'Velvet Queen', quite unlike the sunflowers any of us grew as children, commands full attention with its luxurious brown blooms. The same shape and color, *Helenium* 'Moerheim Beauty' looks like a slighter, more delicately drawn sibling. Bronze fennel, with its flowers of deep amber, is at its fuzziest and haziest at this time of year, adding to the general autumnal feeling of going to seed. *Colutea × media* flowers on beautifully, but now outdoes itself by adding decorative shiny bronze bladderlike seedpods. The hybrid *Dahlia* species will be lifted in late October or early November to make way for the planting of bulbs for spring. Deep orange 'Ellen Houston' and pale orange 'David Howard' both sport dark foliage, so have already been adding color and interest to the border for many months. The color of 'David Howard' is echoed in the flowers of *Asclepias tuberosa*; while the brick-orange trumpets of *Phygelius × rectus* harmonize with *Crocosmia* 'James Coey' and trail a thread of scarlet into this part of the border. With sun shining through them, the nasturtium leaves on the left become juicily translucent.

SPRING

SUMMER

AUTUMN

from top to bottom

TULIPA 'GOLDEN ARTIST'

OENOTHERA VERSICOLOR 'SUNSET BOULEVARD'

COLUTEA × MEDIA

MECONOPSIS CAMBRICA

ROSA 'WESTERLAND'

ASCLEPIAS TUBEROSA

GEUM 'DOLLY NORTH'

POTENTILLA 'WILLIAM ROLLISON'

DAHLIA 'DAVID HOWARD'

FRITILLARIA IMPERIALIS 'THE PREMIER'
ARCTOTIS X HYBRIDA 'FLAME'
LEONOTIS NEPETIFOLIA

EUPHORBIA GRIFFITHII 'FIREGLOW'
ZINNIA SPECIES
HELENIUM 'MOERHEIM BEAUTY'

PAEONIA DELAVAYI X P. DELAVAYI VAR. LUTEA
ESCHSCHOLZIA CALIFORNICA 'DALLI'
TAGETES PATULA

RED spells passion,

the message, unmistakable the impact. Red is stop lights, fire engines, blood. Everyone understands exactly what to expect from red: it attracts attention, it creates drama. Simply looking at this color stimulates the body into an adrenalin rush, in preparation for danger. Physiological studies indicate that red lighting leads to a rise in blood pressure, body temperature and rate of breathing. Little wonder that red is considered a hot color, since it really does create heat. Saturated red has the longest wavelength of any color in the spectrum visible to humans, and invisible infrared waves, next to visible red, actually are heat waves.

Unrestrained and vital, a red border is always a stimulating visual pleasure. For almost a century now, people have scrambled to enjoy the rich red borders of Hidcote Manor garden in Gloucestershire, England, and for decades the sumptuous red border in the late Peter Healing's garden at the Priory, Kemerton, Worcestershire, has attracted the same attention. Many people are as timid about using red as they are about using orange, and caution is often advocated in instructions for designing and planting with such hot colors as these — but why, when instinctively we seek them out? Red need not be fire-engine scarlet, harsh or glaring; red can be moody or voluptuous, as sensuous as silk velvet. Red is altogether too lively and energetic to be treated as the rebel or outsider in color schemes. Of course, knowledge of its personality is essential, of what it does and of how to use it to its fullest potential. Red can add so much to a garden, whether on its own in a monochrome border, or in combination with other, harmonious colors. Those who genuinely shy away from its dynamism might first try using it as an accent in a planting, or in containers, and thus learn to love it.

power and pizzazz — clear is

Red has always been associated with position, importance, riches — the red button on the hat of a mandarin of the first class, the red hat, itself, of a cardinal. In his desire for this significant color, man once went to extraordinary lengths to obtain it, and such were the difficulties involved that it was always expensive. One source was the bodies of dried insects such as the cochineal beetle (*Dactylopius coccus*); another, the roots of plants like madder (*Rubia tinctorum*); a third, dyewoods like brazil-wood (*Caesalpinia echinata*). The insects had to be gathered, the plants cultivated and harvested, the trees felled and chopped before the lengthy process of preparing the dye could even begin. In the mid-nineteenth century, the development of aniline dyes based on coal tar brought red within everyone's reach, but many expressions and color names remain as echoes of its natural origins. Another insect, *Kermes vermilio*, the source of the most ancient recorded dyes, gave its name to carmine, crimson and vermilion, and *red tape* derives from the tape used to bind legal documents together, formerly colored with a dye obtained from safflower (*Carthamus tinctorius*).

According to W. B. Yeats in *Fairy and Folk Tales of the Irish Peasantry*, "Red is the color of magic in every country. . . . The caps of fairies and musicians are well-nigh always red." Leaving magic and fairies (and hats) aside, red, warm and exciting has certainly long been associated in interiors with entertainment, a sense of the theatrical — walls draped in red damask, red velvet stage curtains, the red light of the brothel. The British National Trust range of paints, based on original colors from early properties, includes Picture Room Red, Eating Room Red, and Book Room Red, indicating the wide-ranging domestic use of this color over the centuries.

THE OLD BRICK WALLS OF HADSPEN
MAKE THE PERFECT CANVAS FOR THIS
ARRANGEMENT IN WHICH THE ROSES
'ALTISSIMO' (LEFT) AND 'PARKDIREKTOR
RIGGERS' (RIGHT) FLAME AGAINST THE
TERRACOTTA. THE INTENSE SCARLET RED
OF THE DAHLIA 'BISHOP OF LLANDAFF'
BLAZES AGAINST ITS OWN GLOSSY BLACK
FOLIAGE, AS DRAMATIC IN ITS TONAL
CONTRAST AS CROCOSMIA 'LUCIFER' IS IN
ITS COLOR CONTRAST. GEUM 'MRS
J. BRADSHAW', TROPAEOLUM 'RED WONDER'
AND POTENTILLA 'GIBSON'S SCARLET'
TAKE DOTS OF RED TO THE PATH EDGE.

Using red

The immense power and drama of red can be used to manipulate a space effectively: a small sliver creates an edge, a tension, while a large slash is pure impact. This pure, primary color is best seen at mid- to close range — intimate viewing for the most emotive color — because on the whole it absorbs light, and reflects very little. In a dark or shady border, red will be lost, especially if all the surrounding foliage is dark, and for this reason it is of little use for lending distance or depth to a planting. Keep it close at hand to appreciate its energy to the fullest. A foliage planting of silver or gray provides an impression of light from which red will radiate like a ruby or garnet set in silver.

The purest scarlet is the soul of red, unadulterated by any yellow or blue. Green is the most dominant color in the garden, and red is directly opposite green on the color wheel: together they create a unique vibrancy. Although for success, it is essential to pay attention to the balance between flower and foliage color. As stunning as red is with green, it is sublime when harmonizing with darker red, bronze or coppery foliage. Indeed, many plants in the red palette also have dark leaves, thus contributing to the plan in two ways. The rosettes of dark foliage are one with the sultry brunette flowers of *Dianthus barbatus* Nigrescens Group: when even the leaves stay within the monochrome, the penetrating red dances within the harmony.

Not everything associated with this color need be bold and sassy, but it certainly can be if that is what you want. A planting that includes poppies, dahlias and cannas, all with bold bright blooms, will be assertive and flashy. We adore the oriental poppies simply for their unabashed profusion of color. *Papaver orientale* 'Beauty of Livermere' must take the prize for this, its blood-red petals as glowing and alluring as any lips colored with Chanel's Rouge Coromandel.

Choose plants with many small flowers to create a quieter, Impressionist planting style. The small intensely red flowers of herbaceous *Potentilla*, *Helianthemum* and *Salvia* make a floating haze amid green foliage. This style of planting can be used to re-create a wildflower

... red is sublime when harmonizing with darker red, bronze or coppery foliage ...

meadow, with field poppies (*Papaver rhoeas*), scarlet pimpernel (*Anagallis arvensis*) and pheasant's-eye (*Adonis annua*). The use of color in garden design knows no boundaries: whether it is a windowbox, a border or a bog garden, a shrubbery or a kitchen garden, the same theories apply.

Anyone who has ever read about or used red in the garden will know the name at least of the *Dahlia* 'Bishop of Llandaff'. We too extol the virtues of this wonderful plant, which we first met on Vancouver Island when we gardened for Mary Greig, the great North American rhododendron hybridizer. It was quite a rare plant in that place at that time, and for many years Mary had taken great pains to keep the tubers going. As so often happens in such cases, however, it was becoming increasingly difficult to propagate because of a virus, and indeed was almost lost to horticulture. Thanks to keen-eyed Somerset nurseryman Duncan Travers, who spotted its potential, its current proliferation is one of the great achievements of micropropagation. Using this method clean stocks were obtained, and it is now a healthy, vigorous variety. Although

it is so much easier to obtain and to keep these days, this certainly does not make it any less desirable or valuable to the gardener. Glowing scarlet flowers generously displayed through summer and autumn over bronze foliage with a pewter cast make this a showy plant. We position it with *Crocosmia* 'Lucifer' and *Potentilla* 'Gibson's Scarlet', where it is set off by their sharp green foliage yet blends with their flowers. This enthusiasm for the Bishop should not be taken to mean there are no other equally deserving and beautiful crimson dahlias: every red border could find a place for 'Black Diamond', 'Summer Night', and 'Arabian Night'. Dahlias are from Mexico, so they are great lovers of heat and will do well in a hot and sunny spot; they also grow happily in a container, where they are able to absorb heat from head to toe.

Without question, many of the best shades of red come from the half-hardy perennials and annuals. The red *Salvia*, the darling of the flower-bed brigade, has taken on quite a new look thanks to intrepid plant explorers. The Compton, d'Arcy & Rix expedition of 1991 to

Mexico brought back glorious shades of cerise, vermilion and scarlet in selections of *Salvia x jamensis* (hybrids of *S. microphylla* and *S. greggii*), found growing near Saltillo, northeast of the Sierra Madre Oriental mountain range. These salvias are quite hardy if fed sparingly and kept dry in winter, but it is always best to take cuttings at the end of summer, in case of a hard winter. *Salvia microphylla* 'Cerro Potosi', however, from the same area, is hardy to 5°F.

There are some favorite annuals that we would not want to lack in our red border, including *Nemesia* 'Fireking', for its bright dots of scarlet to crimson; *Tropaeolum majus* 'Red Wonder', a clump-forming selection of the familiar nasturtium which is propagated from cuttings, with a dark emerald-green leaf and semidouble deep red flowers; the brick-red double blooms of *Gaillardia pulchella* 'Red Plume'; and, for foliage as well as flower, *Ricinus communis* 'Carmencita'. All these plants will reward the trouble of growing them from seed and occasional deadheading by adding color and substance to the border for many months.

Position reds where they can bask in late afternoon sun and the long rays of light can warm the backs of flowers and foliage and set them ablaze. Red and copper leaves that have been used to provide a deep, matt background against which to set off flowers will, when lit like this, change to glowing objects in their own right. If it is planted this way, red can be enjoyed twice as much, in quite different ways. At Hadspen we make a point of timing our visits to the red planting so that we can enjoy just this electric charge.

The quintessential red flower is surely the rose. A favorite subject of poets and romantics, it inspires the same passion in the gardener. But let us be clear that here at Hadspen we have nothing to do with the traditional rose garden of hybrid teas, where tortured, stunted, diseased bushes perched in bare earth sometimes produce a flower. These sorts of roses, if required, should be confined to the cutting garden. The roses we recommend for the border are shrubs that give structure and shape to a planting, as well as flowers. From purest scarlet left LOOKING LIKE SOME EXOTIC WADING BIRD, *CROCOSMIA* 'LUCIFER' GIVES PLEASURE IN ALL STAGES OF ITS GROWTH, FROM THE FEATHERLIKE SYMMETRICAL ARRANGEMENT OF ITS BUDS TO THE SCARLET TRUMPET FLOWERS AND FAWN SEEDPODS. ITS HANDSOME FOLIAGE, LIKE GREEN SWORDS FLASHING, COULD ONLY BE UPSTAGED BY ITS DAZZLING FLOWERS.

right *ANTIRRHINUM MAJUS* 'BLACK PRINCE', AN OLD VARIETY OF SNAPDRAGON, COMBINES DARK STEMS AND FOLIAGE WITH VELVETY CRIMSON BLOOMS. THE SINGLE-FLOWERED FLORIBUNDA ROSE 'DUSKY MAIDEN' TAKES ON THE SAME COLOR AND TEXTURE, GENTLY TURNING TO A WINE RED AS IT FADES. THE SILVER-GRAY FOLIAGE OF *CENTAUREA CYANUS* 'BLACK BALL' HIGHLIGHTS ITS OWN DAMSON CORNFLOWERS AS WELL AS LIFTING THE REDS IT SURROUNDS.

left A TEXTURAL MEDLEY OF GREEN
FOLIAGE IS ELECTRIFIED BY THE BACKLIT
CRYSTALLINE CUPS OF *TULIPA* 'RED WING'
AND THE YOUNG FOLIAGE OF *PRUNUS
X CISTENA*. WE PRUNE THIS CHERRY BACK
BY TWO-THIRDS IN LATE WINTER, WHICH
ENCOURAGES VIBRANT COLOR AND
LARGE-SIZED YOUNG LEAVES WHILE ALSO
KEEPING IT TO A TIGHT SHAPE.

right CREPE-PAPER PETALS OF *PAPAVER
ORIENTALE* 'BEAUTY OF LIVERMERE'
CRADLE A THICK CENTER OF BLACK
STAMENS SURROUNDED BY A BLACK
BLOTCH, MAKING THIS THE FINEST RED
ORIENTAL POPPY WE KNOW. THE TALL
UPRIGHT STEMS NEED STAKING, AS THEY
CAN REACH A HEIGHT OF 5 FEET, BUT
MAKE AN IMPOSING STAND ON PARADE
ABOVE THE EXCELLENT FOLIAGE OF
PRUNUS X *CISTENA*.

to deepest crimson, a rose can be found to fit the need. We use fire-engine red 'Altissimo', a superb single rose that is never out of flower, as both a climber and a large shrub; 'Parkdirektor Riggers' offers the same vibrant color in a semidouble climber that is equally willing to flower throughout the season. From the crimson side of red, try the climber 'Guinée', superb in color and scent (it needs some shade to fade well, turning an off-cerise in full sun), or the Floribunda 'Dusky Maiden', similar in color but single flowered. Success in using these roses in a planting depends not only on their capacity for a sustained performance but also on the way they are associated with other shrubs and herbaceous plants. At Hadspen the scarlet shades of the rose 'Altissimo' are mirrored in the shape and color of *Potentilla* 'Gibson's Scarlet' and *Geum* 'Mrs J. Bradshaw'; *Geum* will be in flower from April until July, when *Potentilla* takes over until late summer. As part of a harmonious planting that includes orange and yellow, the yellow stamens of all three will provide an easy transition from red to orange.

The possibilities of red are not bound by the flower garden. The vibrant way tomatoes, radishes and red peppers adorn a dinner plate has never been undervalued, and now red makes its contribution in the kitchen garden. Among the vegetables at Hadspen, we grow rows and plots of lettuces — 'Rosalita', 'Rougette du Midi' and 'Cocarde' — all with beautiful red or red-tinged leaves, to delight the palate and the eye. Heads of radicchio, stalks of ruby chard and flowers of scarlet runner beans all complement one another beautifully. It is always interesting to try some of these vegetables in a traditional border. We use ruby chard in the red border at Hadspen, and of course the beet 'Bull's Blood' in the plum border; as it runs to seed the fleshy red leaves of the lettuce 'Cocarde' look particularly good among *Papaver somniferum*. The fruit garden and the orchard also beckon, with their luscious ripe fruits. Supposedly, clever breeders have achieved only limited success with their attempts to fool birds with white currants and white raspberries: it is true the birds do not want them — but neither do we.

Seasonal progression

SPRING Red is comparatively rare at this time of year, which is just as well as a little goes a long way under the diffused light of spring. An April day is set ablaze by this quartet of tulips, which are more than simply red. The Triumph tulip 'Prominence' shares the front row with 'Red Wing', a fringed tulip, distinct with its crystalline-edged petals. Standing tall toward the back of the border is another Triumph tulip, 'Paul Richter', in pure scarlet, and the lily-flowered tulip 'Red Shine'. Tulips offer an amazing choice of colors, but almost more interesting are the subtle differences between varieties — the riotous muddle of the Parrot, the soft green stripe of the Viridiflora, the perfect elegance of the Triumph. The deep red foliage of *Prunus* x *cistena* bursts forth on its burgundy stems, making a link with the tulips. Apart from these, the most evidence of red is to be seen in the new growth of leaves and stems on the roses; later it seems as though their color is drained away by the blooms. The green foliage of *Hemerocallis*, *Papaver orientale* and *Crocosmia* 'Lucifer' contrasts with the reds to make this planting shimmer in the late afternoon sun.

SUMMER The leaves of *Prunus* × *cistena*, now darker in tone and becoming leathery in texture, show up the scarlet blooms of *Papaver somniferum*. This annual poppy is one of the color selections we have made specifically for this area. After flowering, the handsome seedpods turn a biscuit brown before dispersing thousands of seeds. These germinate quickly but can be easily weeded out of places where they are not wanted. Single-flowered *Potentilla* 'Gibson's Scarlet' is just coming into bloom, timed to coincide with *Hemerocallis* 'Mrs Hugh Johnson', still in bud. These two plants are identical in color, but contrasting in flower and foliage shape. The double crimson *Potentilla* 'Flambeau', on the right, has been in flower for a few weeks and will continue on until August. Pollination is difficult, if not impossible, for most double flowers, so the plant goes on blooming rather than turning to seed — useful for gardeners, but possibly rather frustrating for the plant, and definitely frustrating for the propagator as this sought-after treasure can only be increased by the slow methods of division or basal cuttings.

AUTUMN This melancholy scene is dominated by dark somber leaves. The leaf color and structure of *Prunus* × *cistena* has become very dense and flat, and the plant has almost come to the end of its long stint in a supporting role. The leaves of *Heuchera* 'Bressingham Bronze' shine like oxblood-colored patent leather as the sun strikes them, but the stems and leaves of ruby chard, from a superb new seed strain given to us by Clive Blazy of Digger's Seeds in Australia, look delicious. Enhancing this bewitching setting, the dazzling scarlet flowers of *Dahlia* 'Bishop of Llandaff' exhibit themselves to the full, held above their matt blackish foliage. Content with the cool nights and warm days of autumn, *Dahlia* can remain in flower until a hard frost. *Salpiglossis* 'Chocolate Pot' glows out of the dark, the red in its velvet maroon blooms seeming to leap out as if it is held in a sunbeam. This annual, a recent introduction from Mr. Fothergill's Seeds, is a great new addition to the red palette, providing both texture and color in a plant with a strong constitution for a sunny position. It seems equally happy in containers or in the border.

SPRING

SUMMER

AUTUMN

from top to bottom

CHAENOMELES SPECIOSA

POTENTILLA 'GIBSON'S SCARLET'

CANNA 'ROI HUMBERT'

GEUM 'MRS J. BRADSHAW'

TROPAEOLUM MAJUS 'RED WONDER'

RICINUS COMMUNIS 'CARMENCITA'

TULIPA PRAESTANS 'FUSILIER'

HEMEROCALLIS 'AZTEC'

ROSA RUGOSA

AQUILEGIA VULGARIS VAR. FLORE-PLENO (RED)

ROSA 'LILLI MARLENE'

DAHLIA 'BISHOP OF LLANDAFF'

PAEONIA DELAVAYI

SALPIGLOSSIS 'CHOCOLATE POT'

GAILLARDIA PULCHELLA 'RED PLUME'

VIOLA X WITTROCKIANA (RED)

DIANTHUS BARBATUS NIGRESCENS GROUP

DAHLIA 'ARABIAN NIGHT'

PLUM is sullen

side, an intriguing combination of red, blue and black, the deepest color in the plant palette. Taking on more red, more blue, even more black, it becomes many shades and tones. Claret, maroon, burgundy, mulberry, puce, all fit into this color group. The word *plum* seems to encompass all these tones, however, for the fruits themselves range from the almost black of a sloe or the rich, deep purple of a damson plum to the paler mulberry shades of a Victoria plum. It seems fitting that *plum* also means *first class*, *treasure*, *prize*.

The darker shades of plum are what is really meant by black in flowers, a color plant breeders have spent many a dark hour striving to create. The first breakthrough was probably made by the Dutch in the course of their search for a black tulip during the seventeenth-century craze known as Tulipomania. Unusually colored, striped or multicolored tulips caused such excitement that the entire Dutch economy came to revolve around the tulip trade. Fortunes were made and lost as even unflowered bulbs changed hands for vast sums, and it all ended in a spectacular financial crash. The splendid La Tulipe Noire is one legacy of Tulipomania, and two centuries later, we are still entranced by the black and velvety texture of its cousins 'Black Parrot' and 'Queen of Night'.

Many more dark-flowered plants have been developed since those tulip-mad days, and the quest continues. The sumptuous and bloomy slate grays, maroons and wines of the newest hellebores are current testimony to the prevailing desire for this color, and a good range of plum-colored annuals has been selected over the last few years, including *Centaurea cyanus* 'Black Ball' and *Scabiosa atropurpurea* 'Ace of Spades'. Even the lowly spud rates exotic status in its forms 'Salad Blue', 'German Black' and 'Edgecote Purple'.

and sumptuous, on the dark

This is a color to be viewed very close up — there is little point in placing it to be seen from a distance, as only a black hole appears. In the darkest tones, the saturation is nearly complete, allowing only the smallest amount of red and blue to seep out, as a glance at a purple beech in the landscape will confirm. Little light is reflected from plum; it is absorbed instead, drawing us in. Many flowers of this color also have petals of a velvety texture — the rose 'Souvenir du Docteur Jamain', *Clematis viticella* 'Royal Velours' and *Cosmos atrosanguineus*, for instance — as if their sultry color was not temptation enough. Often the petals of our ancient China rose 'Louis XIV' are to be found bruised and tattered, after a day of fondling by garden visitors.

As with red, textiles and fabrics of plum and purple have long been associated with wealth and opulence, Empire and papacy, because the dyes used were obtained only with great difficulty and expense. The Cretans, Phoenicians, Greeks and Romans knew the secret. The dye for the Tyrian purple of antiquity was extracted from the soft tissue of certain shellfish, notably of the genus *Murex*, and it took eight thousand shells to yield one gram of dye; the secret of its manufacture is now lost. It would be easy to suppose that the color known as murrey must be derived from those shellfish, but it comes rather from the Latin for mulberry, *morus*, and is a quite different shade.

The subdued intensity of plum can be used to design a planting as heavy and gloomy as a Victorian parlor luxuriously furnished with plush Persian carpets, sumptuous velours and rich tapestries. Usually the aim of a plant association is to cheer and enlighten, but there is also a place in the garden for a more inward-looking indulgence, and plum can create an atmosphere of mysterious opulence.

THE FLOATING HEADS OF *ALLIUM ATROPURPUREUM* AND *PAPAVER SOMNIFERUM* DRIFT THROUGH THE BORDER WITH A PAPAL GRACE; AT THEIR FEET IS *POTENTILLA* 'ETNA', WITH PENNY-SIZED FLOWERS. *DIANTHUS BARBATUS* NIGRESCENS GROUP MAKES A BOLDER STAND, WITH VELVETY CRIMSON POSIES HELD ON RUBY STEMS AND FOLIAGE, WHILE *DIANTHUS* 'DAD'S FAVORITE' BOWS TO THE GROUND. THE ROSES 'GUINÉE' (LEFT) AND 'SOUVENIR DU DOCTEUR JAMAIN' (RIGHT) STAND GUARD ON THE WALL; 'CARDINAL DE RICHELIEU' LOOKS POISED TO RECEIVE ADULATION.

Using plum

The luxury of designing planting schemes with plum lies in the availability not only of an exquisite choice of flowers, but of a diversity of foliage as well. Together they have the potential to make some of the most unusual and stunning combinations. A shrub or tree with dark foliage, carefully placed, will give a solid anchoring effect to a planting. The leaf color needs to be precisely balanced with the flowers and green foliage used, otherwise it will obscure the planting, not enhance it. There are shapes and sizes for most situations. We use *Phormium tenax* Purpureum Group, *Corylus maxima* 'Purpurea' with its plummy tassels and nuts, or *Cotinus coggygria* 'Royal Purple'. The nut and the cotinus are cut back in early spring by two-thirds of last year's growth, to encourage larger leaves. An entire planting might be backed by a hedge of *Prunus pissardii* or purple beech, or a wall of deep red-to-maroon brick.

Use this dark shrubby framework as a climbing structure for clematis, especially *Clematis viticella* 'Minuet' with burgundy bands on a cream background, 'Purpurea Plena Elegans' with double dusky maroon rosettes, or 'Madame Julia Correvon' in wine red. All these varieties of *Clematis viticella* are essential for the late summer border as they flower from mid-July on into September. Pruning is simple — cut back all growth to about 1 foot in February. There will be no trouble with the dreaded wilt disease, and their masses of smallish, elegant flowers make these clematis worthy of a place in any planting scheme. If you can keep pace with their rapid spring growth, the trouble taken in training new shoots to grow horizontally by gently bending and tying them — every three days — onto either wires on the wall or the branches of their host plant will be rewarded with an almost embarrassing amount of flower.

A thread of plum-colored foliage to hold a design together can be provided by annuals and perennials. The self-seeder *Atriplex hortensis* var. *rubra* works beautifully in this way, putting itself in clever places that no gardener would ever think of. *Heuchera* 'Bressingham Bronze' and *Dianthus barbatus* Nigrescens Group are quite superb companions for plum-colored flowers, as are some vegetables, in particular the

burgundy-leather-leaved beetroot 'Bull's Blood' or some of the dark-leaved basils — *Ocimum basilicum* 'Dark Opal', 'Rubin' or 'Purple Ruffles'. Such foliage offers color and interest for many months as it grows and matures from early spring to late autumn.

From this foundation planting of foliage, the color can be dispersed through the border using shrubs, herbaceous perennials, annuals and bulbs. Plant bulbs in clumps or drifts to come up through or next to perennials with complementary foliage or flowers. This avoids a regimental parade effect, and the new foliage of the perennials will cover the bulbs' nasty dying leaves. Tulips in glossy, exotic shades of deep wine and warm plum direct the late spring performance. Whether you are able to keep tulips in the ground from year to year will depend on the variety, and how well your soil is drained. On our clay soil we have little success, but having to buy new tulips each season is a good excuse for trying out new varieties. Alliums, the ornamental onions, are great providers for the summer border, and generous plantings will set up

a strong percussion rhythm as their drumstick heads emerge from a mass of herbaceous foliage. The glistening aubergine flowers of *Allium atropurpureum* float above clumps of *Geranium phaeum* 'Samobor' with its chocolate-blotched leaf or the black cow parsley (*Anthriscus sylvestris* 'Ravenswing'), and in late summer *Allium sphaerocephalon* carries on the rhythm with egg-shaped claret-colored heads.

One woman's rubbish is another woman's treasure: *Papaver orientale* 'Patty's Plum' has the most exotic color in this genus in pleated petals of deep mulberry silk, like the fabric of faded ball gowns. We admired this poppy in the garden of Patricia Marrow, a nurserywoman of great repute, who condemned it as dull and muddy and demanded that we dig it up immediately — which we did, and named it after her. Its extraordinary color makes it one of the most important perennials in our plum scheme. Carrying on after the oriental poppies and lending yet more mystique, the opium poppies (*Papaver somniferum*) prance through the garden in all shades and tones. We are particularly fond of the single

left HERE OLD VARIETIES OF DARKNESS, THE *LUPINUS* 'THUNDERCLOUD' AND *DIANTHUS BARBATUS* NIGRESCENS GROUP, ARE SEEN COMBINED WITH SOME OF OUR NEWEST PLANT DEVELOPMENTS. COMING UP THROUGH A CONTINUALLY FLOWERING DARK RED *ASTRANTIA MAJOR* 'HADSPEN BLOOD' AND *PAPAVER ORIENTALE* 'PATTY'S PLUM' ARE *ALLIUM ATROPURPUREUM* AND A GRAY-LEAVED *PAPAVER SOMNIFERUM* WITH THE SAME CLARET-COLORED BLOOMS. SELF-SEEDING CONTINUES THROUGHOUT THE YEAR WITH THE DOUBLE RED *AQUILEGIA VULGARIS* AND *ATRIPLEX HORTENSIS* VAR. *RUBRA*, AND SO TOO DOES THE CREATIVE WEEDING.

right PLUM IS USED HERE TO TURN UP THE VOLUME OF THE PINK EXPERIENCE. PINK REFLECTS THE LIGHT AS PLUM ABSORBS IT – CREATING TONAL CONTRAST. HOT PINK FLOWERS OF *DIANTHUS CARTHUSIANORUM* PEER THROUGH THE FOLIAGE OF *ATRIPLEX HORTENSIS* VAR. *RUBRA*, WHOSE DARK BURGUNDY LEAVES AND STEMS INTENSIFY THE DELICATE PINK SPIRES OF *LINARIA PURPUREA* 'CANON WENT'. SELF-SOWN SEEDLINGS OF *DIGITALIS PURPUREA* OFFER VARYING SHADES OF PINK.

left LIKE THE THREADS OF AN INTRICATE PIECE OF NEEDLEWORK, THE CRIMSON PINCUSHION FLOWERS OF *KNAUTIA MACEDONICA* WEAVE UP INTO THE DOUBLE PLUM FLOWERS OF *PAPAVER SOMNIFERUM* WHILE *GERANIUM* 'ANN FOLKARD' THREADS THROUGH THE STEMS WITH DEEP MAGENTA BLACK-CENTERED FLOWERS. A COMBINATION OF LEAF SHAPES, TEXTURES AND COLORS (GRAY-GREEN, CHARTREUSE AND EMERALD) PROVIDES AN INTERESTING BACKGROUND TO THIS PLANTING.

right TATTERED PETAL EDGES OF *TULIPA* 'BLACK PARROT' MIMIC THE DEEPLY INCISED GRAY LEAVES OF *CYNARA CARDUNCULUS* (CARDOON). THE PERENNIAL WALLFLOWER *ERYSIMUM* 'BOWLES' MAUVE' PROVIDES MASSES OF RICH MAUVE FRAGRANT FLOWERS OVER A LONG PERIOD. UNFORTUNATELY, THE ABILITY TO FLOWER CONTINUOUSLY SEEMS TO CAUSE THIS PERENNIAL TO BE RATHER SHORT-LIVED, SO WISDOM DICTATES THAT YOU ALWAYS HAVE SOME CUTTINGS ON HAND.

and double black forms we have selected over the years. These poppies are notorious for their promiscuity and self-seeding, but with ruthless weeding out of any interlopers, a pure strain can usually be achieved in one or two seasons, depending on how many misfits you already have.

No plum planting scheme would be complete without *Cosmos atrosanguineus* and its burgundy-velvet blooms smelling of chocolate. This cosmos, a perennial species from Mexico, is another micropropagation success. We plant it 6 inches deep and keep it dry in winter under a glass cloche. Many plants on the borderline of hardiness object not so much to the cold conditions of winter as to the wetness.

The roses 'Tuscany Superb', 'Charles de Mills' and 'Nuits de Young' seem redolent of a sultan's tent, stimulating every sense with their sumptuous hues of maroon, crimson and purple, their textures of finest silk and scents of incense and myrrh. If you like Turkish Delight confections, a sip of rose dew really is divine. As one would expect of such august beings, these dark roses enjoy being pampered, with lots of feeding,

selective pruning and training. In the winter we heap piles of farmyard muck around each bush, to mulch as well as to fertilize. Flowering in all our roses is encouraged by training the stems horizontally on a framework made of green bamboo or coppiced willow or ash. This promotes the formation of blooms all along the stems, rather than just at the tips. After the roses have flowered, this framework can do duty as a climbing structure for sweetpeas — speckled 'Wiltshire Ripple' or bicolored *Lathyrus odoratus* 'Matucana' — or *Clematis*.

Plum harmonizes with many colors on either side of it in the spectrum, blue or red. Pinks, magentas and lavenders all feel at home with plum, while the sharpness of scarlet, from *Dahlia* 'Bishop of Llandaff' or *Lobelia* 'Queen Victoria', adds an electrifying element. Since plum absorbs light, using it with whites, silvers and grays creates a delicate tension. It also contrasts beautifully with oranges, yellows and peaches. For a dramatic effect, try *Cosmos atrosanguineus* and rich orange *Tithonia rotundifolia* against a planting of *Berberis* x *ottawensis*.

Seasonal progression

SPRING Dark foliage is mixed with shades of gray and green, its textures and shapes making a rich spring tapestry. Maroon-red *Atriplex hortensis* var. *rubra* seeds happily along the path edge and into the border. The bronze stems and leaves of *Paeonia lactiflora* 'Karl Rosenfeld', like those of many in this genus, are as significant and beautiful as its flowers, adding months to its garden value. Here they take the thread of dark color deep into the border. *Phormium tenax* 'Burgundy' makes a bold statement year-round with its plum-colored, swordlike leaves, linking with the dark foliage of emerging herbaceous plants as well as echoing the leaf shape of the tulips and Germanica irises. Architectural plants like this *Phormium* are important in all seasons, but most valuable in spring. Give it a rich fertile soil in full sun and protect it from harsh winter winds by tying up the leaves. Velvety maroon-black blooms of *Tulipa* 'Queen of Night' tower over the silver-gray foliage of *Artemisia ludoviciana* 'Valerie Finnis' and tulips a tone lighter, name mysteriously unknown, lead the way to the pink section.

SUMMER Tones of plum, wine and maroon in flowers and foliage mingle in this border in early summer. *Papaver orientale* 'Patty's Plum', with magnificent sheer puce-blue blooms, each petal a study in the complex construction of this color, is the prima donna taking center stage; the standards of an unnamed *Iris germanica* of local provenance are identical in color. *Atriplex hortensis* var. *rubra* is now at the stage where the growing tips are pinched out to make a branched plant. At the front of the border, the color of claret wine is provided by a double *Aquilegia vulgaris*, which seeds true to type, and further in by *Knautia macedonica*, its scabiouslike flowers held on thin stems well above the foliage. This choice perennial will be in flower nonstop from May until December. Setting off the thrusting *Iris germanica* 'Black Swan', its near-black blooms glowing incandescent purple in the setting sun, a wispy spray of the tiny white flowers of *Anthriscus sylvestris* 'Ravenswing' almost disappears. On the far right, the rose 'Charles de Mills' is at the ready, in full bud, to proffer perfumed blooms of a luxurious purple-plum mixture.

AUTUMN *Atriplex* now makes a living screen at the path's edge, and the always-moving oval burgundy heads of *Allium sphaerocephalon* peer out through this plum curtain, held well clear of its now dormant foliage on wirelike stems. It spreads with equal vigor in heavy or light soil, wet or dry. *Clematis viticella* 'Rubra' drapes the back wall and clambers up into *Cotoneaster*, covered with masses of small wine-red blooms and ready to flower for many weeks, while *C. viticella* 'Minuet' clings to a wisteria above the doorway. Velvet maroon *Cosmos atrosanguineus* is strategically placed at the edge of the border and in terra-cotta pots around the bench, to bring its chocolate scent within nose reach. Other pots contain *Pelargonium* 'Dark Venus', *Petunia* x *hybrida* 'Able Mabel', *Salpiglossis* 'Chocolate Pot', and the rose 'Louis XIV', with luscious scent and dark blooms. *Lythrum salicaria* towers above the planting, its violet-magenta flowers blending with the nodding heads of the species *Clematis viticella*, which draw this stormy color up the wall and out of the pinks, toward the more mature tones.

SPRING

SUMMER

AUTUMN

from top to bottom

FRITILLARIA MELEAGRIS

ASTRANTIA MAJOR 'HADSPEN BLOOD'

BRACTEANTHA BRACTEATA 'CRIMSON VIOLET'

IRIS GERMANICA 'RUBY CONTRAST'

PAPAVER ORIENTALE 'PATTY'S PLUM'

TRICYRTIS FORMOSANA

TULIPA 'BLACK PARROT'

ROSA 'LOUIS XIV'

ANGELICA GIGAS

EUPHORBIA DULCIS 'CHAMELEON'

HEMEROCALLIS 'LITTLE GRAPETTE'

COSMOS ATROSANGUINEUS

GERANIUM PHAEUM

ALLIUM ATROPURPUREUM

SANGUISORBA OFFICINALIS

HELLEBORUS TORQUATUS PARTY DRESS GROUP

PAPAVER SOMNIFERUM 'DOUBLE BLACK'

PELARGONIUM 'DARK VENUS'

PINK is soothing,

restful to the eye and brain, pleasant and inoffensive, but at the same time such a positive color — pretty in pink, in the pink. Many people use pink in their first gardens, and since the challenge it presents is quite limited, it is a good choice: the result will almost always be agreeable, if never dramatic. Because it is hard to go wrong with this color, confidence gained from using it successfully will engender the courage to experiment with other, stronger colors. At the beginning of their gardening lives, people worry too much about making mistakes; in time, they come to realize that the mistakes are all part of the learning process.

      Pink is a simple pastel, a combination of just two colors, red and white. Although it does not have a place in the standard spectrum, some people — Tricia Guild in her book *On Color*, for one — argue that it is a color in its own right, indicating that the spectrum is more a matter of physics than of perception. Certainly pink is unique among simple pastels in having been accorded a specific name. The white in palest pink is the 'color' linking it with other pastels, the adhesive force. In all pastel hues, both absorption and reflection of light are moderate, because of this white dilution. Depending on how much white it contains, pink encompasses many shades, from the subdued color sometimes known as dawn pink to a flamboyant magenta. This variability makes it adaptable for use with many other colors, both primary and secondary. Pink is versatile: it will shine in the shade, advancing through shadows and deep green foliage, or appear faded or bleached in the sun, giving a feeling of Mediterranean heat even in a soggy damp drizzle. A wide range of plants is available for either situation, from *Dicentra*, *Hellebore* and *Anemone* for the shade to an endless list of sun lovers including *Rosa*, *Dianthus*, *Cistus* and *Iris*.

comfortable, undemanding,

In interior design, pink is often the choice for bedrooms, where it is used to create an ambience of relaxation and calm. The same principles of design apply to outdoor as well as indoor spaces, and the same effect is achieved. As pink brings light to a dark room, so it will lighten a shady corner in the garden. It also carries with it an element of sweetness and frivolity. But beware: just like red, pink has a hot yellow side and a cool blue side, and associating the two can be tricky. The complexities of a combination of such divergent nonprimary elements of the spectrum are so confusing for the eye that they can result in an unsettling experience.

The theatrical aspects of the color come into play with shades like hot pink and magenta. Magenta is another of the aniline dyes, based on coal tar, and was one of the first synthetic dyes to be commercially produced, around 1860. Because it comes from the blue side of red, its effect is to exert the invisible energies of both infrared and ultraviolet, making it the most dynamic shade in this color range. Perhaps it is fitting that it was named after a battle, at Magenta in Lombardy in 1859. Louise Beebe Wilder, who gardened north of New York City in the early years of this century, referred to it as "that besmirched hue — magenta," and devoted a whole chapter to "Magenta the Maligned" in her book *Color in My Garden*, published in 1918. Unfortunately, many gardeners still feel uncomfortable about it, dismissing it as far too strident for their designs. They should instead be grateful: without it, all would be pallid pink. Using this particular shade calls for thought, however; as Mrs Wilder says, it must not be recklessly handled, yet it is a color that can make a tremendous impact as part of a harmonious planting, or when skillfully placed in a planting of contrasts.

TRULY ROSE-PINK, *ROSA* 'GERTRUDE JEKYLL'

SPILLS PETALS AND PERFUME THROUGH

THE BACK OF THE BORDER AS THE DEEPER

PUCE-PINK OF *ROSA* 'MAGENTA' PEEKS IN

FROM THE SIDE. UPRIGHT FLOWER SPIKES

IN VARYING SHADES OF PINK MAKE A

VERTICAL SCREEN ACROSS THE FRONT OF

THE PLANTING — *DIGITALIS PURPUREA* (LEFT),

VERONICA 'PINK DAMASK' (CENTER) AND

LINARIA PURPUREA 'CANON WENT'

SCATTERED ABOUT.

Using pink

Our main focus for pink at Hadspen is a monochrome scheme in the curved border of the walled garden, running between peach and plum. From the peach (pink with yellow) end, we start with blush pink, building up the intensity through rose madder to the full crescendo of magenta (pink with blue) as we approach the plum section. This part of the border is a favorable setting for pink as it is partially shaded and can be viewed from a distance.

Some of the plantings to the front of the border spill out onto the paving. *Geranium* 'Ann Folkard' spends the summer weaving vivid magenta blooms gracefully through all the neighboring plants, while *Geranium sanguineum* makes a neat hummock covered in deep pink flowers; the variety *Geranium sanguineum* var. *striatum* would work equally well where a paler pink was needed. *Dianthus carthusianorum* sends up spikes of deep pink flowers and *Origanum laevigatum* 'Hopleys' offers an aromatic mat of green foliage before its clusters of pink flowers appear in July, to the delight of the bees and butterflies.

To the front of the border and into the middle, plants such as *Digitalis purpurea*, *Lythrum salicaria* 'Blush' and *Verbascum* 'Pink Domino' weave a pattern of spiky uprights that pull the eye from the path level to the top of the wall, like the baton that directs an orchestra. To balance and complement these uprights are the rounded or spherical forms of tulips, perhaps 'Douglas Bader' or 'Bellflower', peonies such as 'Sarah Bernhardt' or 'Albert Crousse', and old-fashioned or modern roses. The dabs of concentrated color these supply are immediately apparent, and an essential part of the pattern.

The colors and shapes are echoed on the walls in a tangle of climbing roses, clematis and honeysuckle. Often the best climbing frame for a plant is a living one, and climbers placed to grow up and entangle with their host and flower at the same time can be very effective. In the combination of *Rosa* 'Blush Noisette' and *Clematis* 'Comtesse de Bouchaud', the blooms are almost identical in color but the shapes are completely different. A succession of flowering could be

left *CLEMATIS* 'COMTESSE DE BOUCHAUD' ENTWINES WITH *ROSA* 'NOISETTE CARNÉE' AS IT CLIMBS TO THE TOP OF THE WALL. GREAT CLUSTERS OF APPLELIKE BLOSSOMS ON THE *ROSA* 'BALLERINA' COMBINE WITH THE FULL-PETALLED BLOOMS OF 'MARY ROSE' TO GIVE A FINE DISPLAY OF SOFT PINK SHADES. SPECKLES OF DEEP PINK *DIANTHUS CARTHUSIANORUM* AND *DIGITALIS PURPUREA* PEER OUT FROM THE SHADOWLIKE FOLIAGE OF *ATRIPLEX HORTENSIS* VAR. *RUBRA.*

right PLANTS WITH ATTITUDE DEFINES THIS BOLD GATHERING OF MAGENTAS DOMINATING PART OF THE PINK BORDER. THE OLD COTTAGE STALWART *LYCHNIS CORONARIA* IS A GREAT ASSET TO THE HERBACEOUS BORDER, IN ITS FLOWER AND FOLIAGE AND IN ITS PROPENSITY TO SELF-SEED. *GERANIUM PSILOSTEMON* SEEMS INTENT ON STEALING THE SHOW, FLOWERING BRIGHTER AND BIGGER THAN LIFE, ITS CENTRAL BLACK DISK CONTRASTING WITH THE SHARP-TONED PETALS. THE ROSE 'TUSCANY SUPERB' PROVIDES A VELVET BACKGROUND, WITH DAVID AUSTIN'S ENGLISH ROSE 'WILLIAM SHAKESPEARE' TO THE LEFT.

arranged by combining the rose with a later-flowering clematis such as C. 'Duchess of Albany' or one of the *C. viticella* varieties, such as 'Little Nell'. Those who find digging holes a strain will be relieved to be able to put two different plants into the same well-prepared spot — made 3 feet deep and wide, with a wheelbarrow-load of manure or compost mixed into the excavated earth. It is important to remember that most plants need growing space for their roots below ground, proportionate to the size they are likely to achieve above ground.

As insistently as a metronome, several different planting styles mark the rhythm through the border. Bottlebrush blooms of *Persicaria bistorta* 'Superba' contrast with flat umbelliferous heads of *Chaerophyllum hirsutum* 'Roseum', opposing shapes of an identical color; a combination that could as easily be provided by the towering spires of *Lythrum salicaria* and the magenta blooms of *Lychnis coronaria*. Sometimes the flower shape remains the same while the tone or shade of pink changes: this can be most simply achieved by choosing plants from the same

genus or species. *Sidalcea malviflora* in a variety of colors and heights is a welcome addition here: 'Elsie Heugh' with silver-pink fringed flowers is charming planted at the front or in the middle of the border, while the deep pink blooms of 'Loveliness' glow from the back of the planting. Hardy geraniums might be another choice for this particular effect; so useful and reliable, their colors range from the delicate pink of *Geranium* 'Ballerina' through the various pinks of *G. endressii* to the rose pinks and hot pinks of *G. macrorrhizum*, which has the added bonus of scented leaves. Once geranium flowers have gone over, the old leaves and flower stalks can be cut back hard; a less drastic approach is to cut out just the old flowering stems. A second flowering often results from this treatment, but at the least, a fresh set of leaves will be produced within weeks.

As green is the contrasting color to red, which it sets off so well, so an almost pastel green, a sage or gray-green, is the contrast to pale pink, maintaining the same tone. This combination could not be better displayed than in the pink Alba roses. One, 'Queen of Denmark',

. . . pink is unique among simple pastels in having been accorded a specific name . . .

has almost too much to recommend it: beautifully quartered tender pink flowers, intense perfume and a weatherproof constitution, all set off by very healthy gray-green foliage. A lime to almost chartreuse green is the balanced contrast to the magenta end of the pink spectrum, and the hardy geranium 'Ann Folkard' cleverly offers this combination, with early spring foliage of chartreuse turning to an acid green as the magenta blooms appear over several months in the summer. *Dicentra spectabilis* 'Goldheart' is another plant that provides almost the exact combination required. It will lend itself beautifully to a spring corner, with trusses of deep pink flowers held over large yellow-green leaves.

Curiously, this combination of dazzling contrasts on one plant is a not uncommon occurrence. There are several yellow- or gold-leaved forms of plants that gardeners often use while despising their pink flowers — *Spiraea japonica* 'Goldflame', *Lamium maculatum* 'Aureum' and *Origanum vulgare* 'Aureum' are three that frequently come under the gun — yet a planting design based on this combination can be exciting.

ALONG THE BORDER ABOVE THE POND,
A PASTEL MEDLEY OF MAUVE, PINK AND
LILAC HARMONIZES IN THIS HOT, WELL-
DRAINED SETTING. A QUEUE OF *ALLIUM
AFLATUNENSE* 'PURPLE SENSATION' HOVERS
ABOVE THE WANDS OF *NEPETA* 'SIX HILLS
GIANT'. SELF-SOWN *AQUILEGIA VULGARIS*
FLOWERS IN A RANGE OF COLORS FROM
PINK TO PURPLE, AND ITS FOLIAGE
CONTRIBUTES A TEXTURAL PATTERN OF
GREENS AND GRAYS.

No other genus offers so many shades of pink as the rose —
but what precisely is the color rose pink? Rose names in themselves are
seductive, reading like an invitation list to a Bacchanalian summer party
— 'Fantin-Latour', 'Belle Amour', 'Maiden's Blush' — quite apart from their
heady perfume and sumptuous blooms. At Hadspen we are particularly
fond of the shrub roses, not only for these attributes but also for the
way they give almost immediate structure to a planting. With a mixture
of old-fashioned roses, modern shrub roses and English roses, the
flowering season can be extended well into the autumn.

And yet, despite all these attributes, people still demand more
from a rose. It is fair enough to demand scent — once tantalized by the
perfume of 'Madame Isaac Pereire' or 'Zéphirine Drouhin', who would
settle for less? Yet how many hybrid rhododendrons have scent? Only
a repeat-flowering rose is held to deserve space in the garden — but
where are the repeat-flowering camellias? Disease-free roses are another
concern, and justifiably so — but the first step to healthy plants of any

and every genus is a sound program of good nutrition, watering, and pruning if necessary, combined with varieties chosen because they are not susceptible to disease. What other single genus can provide species or hybrids suitable for use as specimen shrubs, hedges, ground cover, climbers, in the borders, in the cutting garden, in the woodland or at the seashore? Short of singing and dancing, the rose has it all. And he who has no roses in his garden has no romance in his soul.

With their gray-green foliage, *Lavandula*, *Artemisia* and *Stachys* all show off pinks to advantage. On the south-facing terrace above our lily pond, the emphasis is on enhancing the Mediterranean air of the setting. Faded shades of pink combine with other pastels, gray-greens and silvers to give the impression of a hot, dry landscape. Lavender-blue *Nepeta* 'Six Hills Giant', cerise *Salvia buchananii*, dusky-pink *Phlomis italica*, rose-pink *Centaurea bella* and mauve *Salvia sclarea* var. *turkestanica* all blend harmoniously because of the white element in their coloring. Fortunately, many plants with pink flowers also have gray or silvery foliage, as well

adapted to set off the color as to a hot, well-drained situation. Selection is almost too easy, and *Dianthus*, *Cistus* and *Centaurea*, like many of the others, have scents to match the ambience.

At Hadspen we encourage self-seeding, merely weeding selectively as necessary. Along with *Linaria purpurea* 'Canon Went' in the pink section of the curved border we welcome *Digitalis purpurea*, from dark pink to the palest flesh tone of 'Sutton's Apricot', and *Papaver somniferum* in transparent shades of pink. These plants pull the composition together, always situating themselves perfectly. Allowing plants to self-seed is a way of discovering new, exciting colors, a more vigorous form, or hardier or more drought-resistant strains. Some of the decorative seedheads contribute as much as the flowers do, while plants like *Papaver somniferum*, *Erigeron karvinskianus* and *Eschscholzia californica* dislike being transplanted, so are best left to sow themselves. Care must be taken not to disturb the tiny seedlings when mulching or weeding in spring, and they can be thinned as they mature.

left THIS SECTION OF THE PINK BORDER
HAS THE AIR — ALMOST THE FLAVOR —
OF A SUGARY CONFECTION. *PAPAVER
ORIENTALE* 'DIANA' IS THE FOCAL POINT,
WITH AMPLE PALEST PINK PETALS HELD
TOGETHER BY A MAROON CENTER.
CANDY-STRIPED *ROSA* 'VARIEGATA DI
BOLOGNA' LOOKS LIKE THE SWEETEST
BONBON IMAGINABLE, WHILE THE PASTEL
SHADES OF *PIMPINELLA MAJOR* 'ROSEA'
ENVELOP THE PLANTING LIKE COTTON
CANDY.

right THE SHOCKING-PINK YET ELEGANT
SPIRES OF THE SPECIES GLADIOLUS,
G. COMMUNIS SSP. *BYZANTINUS*, WHICH IS
MUCH MORE REFINED AND HARDIER
THAN THE LARGE HYBRIDS, ARE RADIANT
AS THEY CATCH THE LIGHT OF THE LATE
AFTERNOON SUN. FROTHY MAUVE-PINK
BLOOMS OF *THALICTRUM AQUILEGIIFOLIUM*
ECHO THE COLOR AND TEXTURE OF
ALLIUM AFLATUNENSE 'PURPLE SENSATION'
AT THE BACK OF THE PLANTING.

SPRING

EARLY SUMMER

Seasonal progression

SPRING Tender and gentle, soft and unassuming, pink fits perfectly into the awakening of this season of hope and promise. In late spring the border is afloat with a collection of *Papaver orientale*. The silky mulberry of 'Patty's Plum' thickens into the ointment pink of 'Blue Moon'. Contrasting with these daubs of color, toward the back of the border stand, on the left, towering deep pink spikes of *Digitalis purpurea* and, in the middle, the vibrant magenta of *Gladiolus communis* ssp. *byzantinus*. Green and pink tutus of *Aquilegia vulgaris* 'Nora Barlow' dance through the planting, adding an element of playfulness. An exotic cousin of *Allium*, *Nectaroscordum siculum* ssp. *bulgaricum* has drooping waxy flowers of similar coloring to *Aquilegia*, and the mellow pink brick wall with its powdery patches of lichen completes the scene.

EARLY SUMMER Pink is the potency of summer roses, modern and old-fashioned, rose-pink, filling the warm air with their perfume. 'Magenta' makes a magnificent mound with blooms of palest pink shadowed slightly

darker and a perfume of pure myrrh, while 'Reine des Violettes', the epitome of an old-fashioned rose with flat, quartered, scented blooms of a violet-pink, blends with velvety maroon-violet 'Tuscany Superb'. *Knautia macedonica* intensifies the pink with deep crimson dots. A thread of magenta is pulled through the border from *Geranium sanguineum* at the path edge to G. 'Ann Folkard' midway and on to *G. psilostemon*, which vies with the tall spires of *Digitalis*. In the middle the darkest ultraviolet *Lupinus* 'Witchet', a seed selection of 'Thundercloud' from Sticky Wicket in Dorset, is a reminder that the plum border is just out of sight.

SUMMER The elegant, pale pink spears of *Veronica* 'Pink Damask' are so pure and delicate, it is a surprise to find them on such a robust and carefree plant. Next to it, the taller spires of that excellent self-seeder *Linaria purpurea* 'Canon Went' look at first glance to be the same: the variations are so slight that the eye slips from one plant to the other. *Cichorium intybus* var. *roseum* balances the scheme with its light pink daisy

flowers borne on tall spikes. All three will flower for weeks. Deeper pinks of *Dianthus carthusianorum*, *Cosmos bipinnatus* and wine-red *Clematis viticella* 'Rubra' combine with the deep leaden claret of *Atriplex hortensis* var. *rubra*, linking the pink border to the plum.

AUTUMN Deep tones of *Atriplex*, now in seed, blend with the dusky pink of *Eupatorium purpureum* 'Purple Bush', a fine selection from the Dutch nurseryman Piet Oudolf, which is larger in flower and taller than the species. The same pink is replicated in the ornamental oregano *Origanum laevigatum* 'Herrenhausen'. A pink form of *Anemone hupehensis* var. *japonica* and the annual *Cleome hassleriana* reach their blooms up into the dark foliage of *Clerodendrum bungei*, which we grow like a herbaceous plant, cutting it right back each spring, and *Sambucus nigra* 'Guincho Purple'. This elder can also be cut back in spring, to two bud sets on each main branch, which will encourage large dark leaves, or it can be left alone to produce its pale pink flowers.

SPRING

SUMMER

AUTUMN

from top to bottom

MALUS DOMESTICA 'GOLDEN RUSSET'

ROSA 'FELICIA'

PHLOX PANICULATA 'MOTHER OF PEARL'

TULIPA 'BELLFLOWER'

GERANIUM SANGUINEUM VAR. *STRIATUM*

SAPONARIA OFFICINALIS 'RUBRA PLENA'

DARMERA PELTATA

CONVOLVULUS ALTHAEOIDES

ANEMONE HUPEHENSIS 'HADSPEN ABUNDANCE'

AQUILEGIA VULGARIS 'NORA BARLOW'
LEUZEA CENTAUROIDES
HIBISCUS SYRIACUS

DICENTRA SPECTABILIS
ROSA GALLICA 'VERSICOLOR'
ROSA 'ZÉPHIRINE DROUHIN'

HELLEBORUS ORIENTALIS
LYCHNIS CORONARIA
SALVIA INVOLUCRATA 'HADSPEN'

PEACH is pure

delicious, a combination of combinations. This variability gives tones and shades of melon, shrimp, salmon and apricot: a gourmet summer menu for the table, or the garden. Mixing red with white to give pink and then adding yellow makes faded peach tints, but mixing red with yellow to give orange and then adding white yields more piquant shades. Such a complexity of hues means peach is diverse enough to combine with many colors to create interesting associations. Like the other pastels, peach is easily seen from a distance, yet its subtle charms can best be taken in at nose length. Its opalescent mother-of-pearl quality can be much more effective in a planting than is a flatter, more saturated primary or secondary color. It seems to add a three-dimensional, reflective element that sets a border shimmering.

Peach is a compelling color in the garden, lending a unique lightness that neither pink nor yellow will provide; it can also be capricious and challenging. One would assume that peach could be slipped in to perform like any other pastel — to harmonize with gray and silver, create an exciting contrast with dark shadowy foliage, or to be enjoyed simply for its own pleasant and subtle appeal. Yet in some situations, the relationship and balance of the white with the red or yellow of peach will determine whether such a substitution works or not. When combining peach with gray, for instance, the peach must not be muted with too much white, otherwise so much light will be reflected from the composition that the definition of the color will be lost, and the result will be insipid. Peach combines most successfully and harmoniously with red and yellow, and with derivatives from, and combinations of, the two. On the other hand, peach will clash with the cool blue-pinks, resulting in associations most eyes will see as downright nasty.

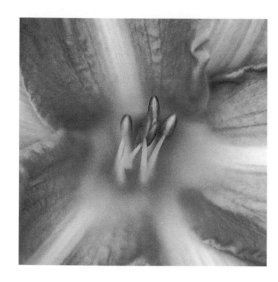

perfection — complex and

Given peach's potential for really antagonistic clashes — such as the creamy tones of annual apricot stocks bullied by the melon of *Hemerocallis* 'Children's Festival', or the almost fluorescent salmon of *Impatiens* repressed by the dainty hues of *Potentilla* 'Daydawn' — an efficient way of grading colors tonally is needed. A method we use here was invented by Pam Lewis, gardener and designer at Sticky Wicket in Buckland Newton, Dorset, England, a great inspiration to us and many others. A collection of flowers of the same color range is assembled on a tray, at intervals throughout the year: it is much easier to mix and shuffle the colors on a tray than to move plants once established in the border. On an expanded scale, plants in pots can be temporarily inserted in the border, to see how a scheme works; this echoes Gertrude Jekyll's ploy of having a cast of plants in pots flowering on the sidelines, ready to be plunged into a border to fill any gaps.

Tricia Guild states that "Peach, especially in its recent, more fashionable manifestations, can be remarkably insipid, the result of omitting the essential element of earthiness." Peach depends for its charm and refinement on an uneven blend of its component colors, and the effect that this unevenness creates. A supersmooth Sheetrock wall painted in flat, commercially mixed peach has as much appeal as a synthetically dyed polyester frock: the evenness and flatness leave both lifeless. By contrast, rough plaster walls washed or stippled with a naturally pigmented paint will have the same depth and luster as a piece of raw silk, in which the uneven weave and the slub take the dye in an irregular and interesting way. Fortunately, in the garden, the natural tonality of peach flowers gives interest and variation; brick, stone, wood and the natural mixture of foliage providing the earthiness with which to enhance this color.

Using peach

Peach once vied with black as the most elusive and sought-after color for the garden; nowadays every seed catalog proudly announces new single-color selections or introductions in the peach range, such as *Salvia coccinea* 'Coral Nymph', described by Suttons Seeds as award-winning, Thompson & Morgan's new and superb *Antirrhinum* 'Peaches & Cream', or Mr. Fothergill's *Aster* 'Apricot Giant', reputed to be of a quite delicious and novel color. If you want a pastel color, peach will usually do very nicely as a pleasant but less predictable alternative to pink or mauve, to be used in much the same way but bringing an element of subtlety and change to a planting.

Because of its complex composition, peach, in its vast range of tints and hues, can be used to enhance many planting areas. Use it in the Mediterranean type of planting — hot, sunny and well drained — discussed in the pink chapter, substituting *Verbena* 'Peaches and Cream' for pink or mauve forms. An excellent assortment of peach *Diascia* is available — 'Salmon Supreme' or, even prettier, 'Blackthorn Apricot' or

'Hopleys Apricot', and they will give many months of pleasure. In a gravel garden, *Verbascum* is a natural. It loves the conditions of good drainage, mulch to the roots and plenty of space to live without any competition, and will provide a dominant line of definition. The ruddy-buff *Verbascum* 'Helen Johnson' and the tawny puce-peach of *V. phoeniceum* 'Cotswold Beauty' will thrive in this situation, and a buff or yellow gravel will set them off particularly well. At the opposite extreme, in a damp boggy planting, *Rodgersia* 'Parasol', the most dramatic of these noble plants, carries a tall, peachy spray of flowers. Echo this flower shape with a planting of *Heuchera micrantha* var. *diversifolia* 'Palace Purple' at its feet, or with great drifts of Himalayan *Primula*, *P. japonica*, *P. pulverulenta* and *P. bulleyana*.

When it comes to a shady dell, the deciduous *Rhododendron* — *Azalea* — will provide a fine color selection. Unfortunately, our alkaline clay soil at Hadspen is anathema to all ericaceous plants, but in our rainforest garden on Vancouver Island's acid soil, they thrived. We sadly

left MASSES OF SMALL PEACHES-AND-CREAM-COLORED FLOWERS COVER THE SHRUBBY *POTENTILLA FRUTICOSA* 'DAYDAWN' FOR MANY WEEKS. WE USE THE TEXTURE, COLOR AND PHYSICAL STRENGTH OF BRONZE FENNEL TO PLAY THE SUPPORTING ROLE WITH *ACHILLEA* 'SALMON BEAUTY'. LONG THIN STRANDS OF *CAREX FLAGELLIFERA*, WHICH GROWS AS IF FASHIONED INTO A HUMMOCK, MAKE AN INTERESTING ASSOCIATION BETWEEN FOLIAGE AND FLOWER.

right A HARMONIOUS PUCE, PINK AND PEACH LIGHT GLEAMS THROUGH SOFT BROWN-PINK FLOWERS OF *VERBASCUM* 'HELEN JOHNSON' ENTANGLED WITH IRREPRESSIBLY CHEERY *DIASCIA* 'SALMON SUPREME'. CONTINUALLY FLOWERING AND ADAPTABLE *ALONSOA WARSCEWICZII* 'PEACHY-KEEN' DEFINES THIS ELUSIVE SHADE.

miss their color and scent, but their absence does not stop us dreaming: we long to design azaleas and other rhododendrons into a harmonious plan including bulbs and other woodland plants, setting the scented *Rhododendron luteum* (formerly *Azalea mollis*) hybrids under a late spring canopy of *Cercidiphyllum japonicum*, whose new leaves are a delicate shrimp-pink, underplanting them with *Epimedium*, *Pulmonaria* and *Aquilegia canadensis*. As the late Dame Sylvia Crowe wrote in *Garden Design*, "There are certain plants, magnificent in themselves, which constantly suffer misuse, and perhaps chief among them are azaleas and rhododendrons." Unfortunately, it seems to be almost a rule that in a rhododendron garden, burning scarlet is teamed with purple and the two juxtaposed with orange, to start spring off with loud firework effects.

Flowers are sometimes bicolored pink and yellow, giving an impression of peach, which can be a great bonus when, as at Hadspen, peach is used to blend through the spectrum from pink to yellow. Several of the honeysuckles are like this, while in some members of the daisy family, the stamens or centers of yellow against pink petals read as peach at a distance. The almost harlequin appearance of the rose known as 'Tipo Ideale' (*Rosa* x *odorata* 'Mutabilis'), with buds of orange opening to pale apricot and fading to coppery pink, makes it a beautiful complement to a peach scheme; challenging, too, since all these colors appear on the bush at once. It is always changing, appearing to be all deep pink at one time, all peach another.

When it comes to choosing a rose of peach tones, the gardener must be content with relatively modern ones, as the breeding of yellow into roses (which led to peach) did not become possible until 1830, when a yellow Noisette rose was created by crossing 'Blush Noisette' with 'Parks's Yellow Tea-scented China' (*Rosa* x *odorata* 'Ochroleuca'), giving rise to peach-colored climbing roses such as 'Gloire de Dijon' and 'William Allen Richardson'. Yellow was introduced into shrub roses in 1900 courtesy of Mr. Pernet-Ducher, of France, who launched 'Soleil d'Or', a cross between a seedling of the Hybrid Perpetual 'Antoine

Ducher' and a seedling of *R. foetida* 'Persiana' crossed with other Hybrid Tea roses — an achievement all gardeners are grateful for, apart from the introduction of black spot that came with it from *R. foetida*. Among older roses 'Buff Beauty' (1939), with clusters of double blooms of rich apricot fading to yellow, 'Mrs. Oakley Fisher' (1921), with single petals of rich apricot, and 'Alchemist' (1956), with swirls of egg-yolk yellow fading to apricot at the edges, are all contenders for inclusion in a peach border. More recently, David Austin's hybridization program has introduced many sumptuous peach-toned English Roses. These require hot summers, hard pruning and heavy feeding to do their best. A mixed bowl of 'Evelyn', 'Charles Austin' and 'Abraham Darby' is pure ambrosia, but all these peach-colored roses are as luxurious as the finest silken froufrou ever seen in Madame de Pompadour's boudoir. Let us praise these colors as Vita Sackville-West did when she saw them in the carpets of the Orient: 'Rich, rich they were, rich as a fig broken open, soft as a ripened peach, freckled as an apricot, coral as a pomegranate.'

It pays to be light-handed in weeding out self-seeders: an inspired color combination can be the result of a happy accident. We had long enjoyed the fine harmony of peach flowers against the bronze foliage of *Sambucus nigra* 'Guincho Purple', *Carex flagellifera* and *Phormium tenax*, but when a seedling of the much redder-leaved *Atriplex hortensis* var. *rubra* lodged itself next to *Achillea* 'Salmon Beauty' we saw how red could lift peach. This same dark color also works well in a flower, the puce of *Papaver orientale* 'Patty's Plum' making an intriguing partnership with *Verbascum phoeniceum* 'Royal Highland', the engaging plum eye of *Verbascum* providing a link between the two.

Peach, the pastel form of orange, also combines well with blue, superbly set off by the cool tones — indigos, purples and plums — like the drama of late afternoon winter skies. For quieter associations, use the pastel blues — pale *Salvia patens* 'Cambridge Blue' with *Alonsoa warscewiczii* 'Peachy-keen', lilac *Buddleja davidii* 'Nanho Blue' with the rose 'Buff Beauty', or lavender *Nepeta* x *faassenii* with *Diascia* 'Salmon Supreme'.

left THE NAME 'CHARMING' PERFECTLY SUITS THE DELICATE STRUCTURE AND SOFT PEACH COLORING OF THIS *PAPAVER ORIENTALE*, BUT LIKE MANY OTHER SOFT CREATURES, IT HAS A WILL AND CONSTITUTION OF IRON. THE *LUPINUS* 'PEACH' IS A SELECTION WE MADE FOR PRECISELY THIS SPOT: BICOLORED YELLOW-PINK, IT GIVES JUST THE DESIRED IMPRESSION, AND DOES SO WITH A SHIMMER. THE HUGE GRASSLIKE LEAVES OF COPPER-GREEN *PHORMIUM TENAX* MAKE A TONAL AND TEXTURAL DOWNSHIFT AWAY FROM THIS FLOWERY SCENE.

right THE TULIP 'APRICOT BEAUTY' IS MORE OF A PEACH MELBA COLOR TO OUR WAY OF THINKING, BUT IT IS INDEED A BEAUTY — EVERYTHING ONE WANTS IN A TULIP, THE SCALE OF FLOWER TO STEM AND LEAF BEING JUST SO. THE COMPLEXITY OF THE BISCUIT GREEN 3-FOOT STRANDS OF *CAREX FLAGELLIFERA* MAKES AN IDEAL TONAL CONTRAST, WHILE HOLDING SEVERAL COLOR HARMONIES WITH PEACH.

Seasonal progression

EARLY SPRING In this bare-legged spring scene, late afternoon sun casts a peach glow on trunks, stems and the brick wall. *Tulipa* 'Apricot Parrot', seen beyond *Papaver orientale* 'Charming' mimicking the shape of the poppy's hairy foliage, looks good enough to eat — as does another, *T.* 'Apricot Beauty', this one sculpted from peach melba ice cream, peering out from behind textural mounds of *Carex flagellifera*. This grass with its mop of fawn strands could be the star in a necrophiliac's garden, as its color often leads people to wonder whether it is dead. When they ask 'What does this grass do?', we reply 'It is doing it.' The most ordinary practicalities have their own beauty when executed with neatness and skill, as the gardeners of our grandfathers' day well knew. Green canes of bamboo, cut fresh from a stand of *Phyllostachys* in the garden, are used to make supports for *Rosa* 'Alchemist', encouraging every shoot along the horizontal stems to bear flowers rather than leaves. Training and tying climbing and rambling roses horizontally against a wall, as we have done with 'Meg' here, will give the same result.

SPRING The aptly named *Lupinus* 'Peach' displays the complexity of the color: the yellow lip, cream gullet and pink hood make up the essence of what it is to be peach. It is placed to complement the subtle coral-edged gray leaves and stems of a tree peony, which waits to unfurl its exotic blooms the same color as the lupin. *Papaver orientale* 'Charming' stands proud, about to unfold papery shrimp-colored blooms. *Iris* 'Holden Clough' is a vigorous cross between a velvety indigo-violet *I. chrysographes* and a pale yellow *I. pseudacorus*. A darkly veined amber of exquisite charm, it nestles behind the *Carex flagellifera*. Clumps of attractive ferny foliage of the giant yarrow (*Achillea chrysocoma* 'Grandiflora'), also behind *Carex*, will soon be accompanied by large cream flowers that turn a biscuit brown as they age.

SUMMER The pink of *Linaria purpurea* 'Canon Went', the incredibly healthy *Rosa* 'Sally Holmes' with its plethora of pale pink buds opening to single buff-cream blooms and the fragrant blossoms of apricot stocks all blend in their color from the pink planting. The darker tones of terracotta, introduced by spires of *Verbascum* 'Helen Johnson', are dusted over *Achillea* 'Salmon Beauty' (midborder) before reaching *Rosa* 'Meg' on the wall. A drop more apricot is found in the stronger shades of *Hemerocallis* 'Peach' and *Potentilla fruticosa* 'Daydawn' at the path edge. *Potentilla* has already been in flower for several weeks, and colors best with some shade. Shear over all the shrubby *Potentilla* plants each spring, reducing by a third, to keep them tight and dense. The frothy apricot flowers of *Macleaya microcarpa* 'Kelway's Coral Plume' are held over handsome gray foliage, which provides an architectural presence at the back of the border. By hard pruning in March, the translucent copper-peach foliage of *Cotinus coggygria* 'Grace' is kept in its large, juvenile phase of growth and blends with the deep plum leaves of *Corylus maxima* 'Purpurea'. The electric chrome-yellow of *Ligularia* 'The Rocket', *Lysimachia punctata* and *Hemerocallis thunbergii* shine out of the shadows, beckoning us on toward the yellow border.

SPRING

SUMMER

AUTUMN

from top to bottom

IRIS GERMANICA 'EDWARD OF WINDSOR'

ALCEA RUGOSA

CALLISTEPHUS CHINENSIS 'APRICOT GIANT'

LONICERA CAPRIFOLIUM

ROSA 'ALCHEMIST'

KNIPHOFIA 'APRICOT'

TULIPA 'APRICOT PARROT'

MACLEAYA MICROCARPA 'KELWAY'S CORAL PLUME'

HEMEROCALLIS 'CHILDREN'S FESTIVAL'

POTENTILLA FRUTICOSA 'DAYDAWN'

MALVASTRUM LATERITIUM

POTENTILLA X HOPWOODIANA

ACTINIDIA DELICIOSA

PAPAVER ORIENTALE 'CEDRIC MORRIS'

HELIANTHUS ANNUUS

LUPINUS 'PEACH'

VERBASCUM 'HELEN JOHNSON'

DAHLIA SHERFFII X D. COCCINEA 'AMBER'

WHITE glows

silver, it gleams in the half-light, giving back more light than it receives, because it has the property of being able to bend invisible ultraviolet and infrared light into the visible spectrum. Add to this the fact that black-and-white vision is one thousand times more sensitive than color vision — a statistic that gives a very good indication of the relative importance of white, both in its pure form and when mixed with other colors to give pastels — and it is easy to see why a white garden is so fantastic in the light of the moon. The white, making no demands on the cones of the eye, gives the rods their time of triumph — perfect for vampires, and other romantic walkers in the dark.

The silvery color and texture of plants, usually most apparent on their leaves, results from the reflection of light from millions of tiny hairs — much as velvet glows and glistens in candlelight. These hairs stop wind and sun from reaching the *stomata* (minute, porelike orifices) on the leaf surface and drying them out. Hairy-leaved plants are, therefore, ideally suited to cope with the sunny, dry and windy parts of the garden. The other side of this coin is that silvery, hairy-leaved plants are so evocative of such conditions that a garden planted with them reads as dry and sunny. Mediterranean, dry and gravel gardens all make use of this perception, and it is strong enough to overcome even the gray skies and drizzle of an English or Pacific Northwest summer.

This silvery quality has in common with gray an ability to harmonize with all other colors. For example, the perfect silver leaves of *Elaeagnus angustifolia* Caspica Group complement both the purple leaves of *Berberis* x *ottawensis* and the blue flowers of *Geranium pratense* with equal ease, and the orange-clawed flower of *Lotus berthelotii* rests sublimely in its own silver foliage.

fluorescent: like gray and

Grayness in leaves is caused by small beads of wax, another way by which certain species protect themselves from dehydration. Like white and silver, gray contains all colors — but in the case of gray, it is a mixture, as if you had tipped all your paints into one pot and stirred them together. White and silver, on the other hand, are caused by an absence of pigment but a reflection of light — which contains all colors. Gray has many coats: the cool blue-gray of *Mertensia simplicissima* or *Cerinthe major* 'Purpurascens' are at the other end of the spectrum from the warm gray of *Macleaya cordata*, while the muddier tones of gray, also warm, move toward puce. It is hard to think of a color to clash with gray; even the Day-Glo magenta flowers of many Mexican cactuses — such as the *Opuntia*, prickly pear — are perfect against it, while the coral candelabra of *Cotyledon orbiculata* is impossible to imagine with any other backdrop. The ubiquitous gray suit has its raison d'être: the color demands little, combines with any surroundings, and enhances the form of its wearer.

The Scandinavians, highly sensitive to the light of their landscape, pick up the opalescent quality of their gray seas and silvered skies, and take these outdoor colors indoors. Interiors painted in such warm, variously toned grays not only maximize the light from the low-angled sun but have the feeling of extending toward the horizon. These colors, so universally effective and popular in northern climates, are known as Gustavian grays, after Gustavus III and IV, kings of Sweden at the end of the eighteenth century.

An all white, silver and gray composition has the potential to be blindingly boring — it would be hard to resist the temptation to sneak in a yellow streak or a flash of *Zauschneria* orange against such a fantastically neutral stage set.

Using white

The many white gardens endlessly written about, even occasionally achieved, stem no doubt from the fact that so many plants have a white-flowered form. Before anyone rushes out to add to the number, please note that very often white flowers die badly — their petals turn brown and cling to the plant instead of dropping off. Brown petals are scarcely noticeable in a pink or orange flower, but on a white one they spell ruination — off they must come.

Although seemingly similar, white, silver and gray have very different uses in design. Smaller white flowers weaving in among other colors will give them a lift and energy that physically brighten the picture, while the white haze created by such flowers as *Crambe cordifolia* or *Anthriscus sylvestris* throws an intriguing veil over the subjects behind. Rather than being usable as a tool to combine disparate color combinations, white in any quantity seems to draw a line through the landscape, becoming a gash of negative space, a separator. When juxtaposed to white, other colors gain in importance by virtue of their contrast with it. In the white garden, the lightest touch is necessary when drawing attention to any nonwhite plant or object. The warming yellow stamens of the ephemeral *Romneya coulteri* or the infrared landing platform in the hollow of a fragrant bloom of *Philadelphus* 'Belle Etoile' alter the whole mood of dominant white.

In an all-white room, the eye will fix upon the slightest anomaly in texture, color or tone. The most subtle detail will stand out in a white room, or a white landscape — so it had better be good. Being alive to the significance white imparts should lead to an increased awareness of the smallest changes. Japanese gardeners in the Classical tradition have a strong sense of this — a plant or stone, well placed against a pale gravel plain, attains the importance of a forest or a mountainscape.

Even in our plantings here at Hadspen where white, silver and gray predominate, it is the anomalies that focus attention on details that might otherwise be missed — such as the burgundy splash at the heart of *Cistus ladinifer*. In the larger view, since silver will read as being at a

distance, *Populus alba* planted on the skyline will be seen as an extension of the horizon. A bank of the most silvery *Elaeagnus angustifolia* Caspica Group, and fronted with *Anaphalis margaritacea* var. *yedoensis* will give a glistening wall with which to screen out any parts of that borrowed landscape which would be better given back. Try such a planting with the red of *Embothrium*, which will appear to leap into your lap out of the retiring background of gleaming mounds.

Bulb foliage can be used to great advantage. The dove-belly grays of new tulip leaves are an ideal foil for their later colors, and the leaves of irises, in particular of *Iris germanica* but above all of *Iris pallida*, provide a similar gray, in perfectly formed blades. Matchless, however, are those of a plant without fault, *Nectaroscordum siculum* ssp. *bulgaricum*: it emerges early, its slug-proof, spatula-shaped buds rising out of the ground like so many silly characters from a Dr. Seuss book; its flowers resembling *Allium*, are rabbit- and deerproof, and we have never seen one insect marked; and they die gracefully. Who could ask for more?

It is notable, too, how many of the most engagingly architectural plants are gray, from *Melianthus* and *Yucca* to *Eucalyptus* and olive trees. Even the ubiquitous *Pyrus salicifolia* can become monumental in the hands of Piet Oudolf, who shapes them into great clipped pillars. This color and the plant life that provides it always play a strong supporting role — as, for instance, the theatrical boost given by the broad gray leaves of *Hosta* 'Snowden' to the simplicity of *Iris sibirica* 'White Swan', setting off the sculpted flower like a diamond in a ring. Indeed, the hostamania that swept Britain and America a decade or so ago was largely fueled in its early stages by Eric Smith and the many hybrids he produced at Hadspen between *Hosta tardiflora* and *H. tokudama*, intensifying the gray-blue coloring of this useful tribe with such well-known varieties as 'Halcyon', 'Hadspen Blue' and 'Blue Wedgwood'.

Silver-foliaged plants are not merely capable of coping with wind and sun, but actively need such conditions; in damp or shady situations the leaves soon lose their sheen, and the plant becomes prone to

left THE GREAT ADVANTAGE OF *ERYNGIUM GIGANTEUM*, ALSO KNOWN AS 'MISS WILLMOTT'S GHOST', IS THAT ALTHOUGH IT IS A BIENNIAL, ONCE YOU HAVE IT IN THE GARDEN IT WILL SEED ITSELF IN CRACKS AND CREVICES. ITS SPECTRAL QUALITY WORKS WELL WITH THE SILVER-GRAY OF *GERANIUM PRATENSE* 'MRS. KENDALL CLARK' AND THE FRAGRANT WHITE ROSE 'MARGARET MERRIL'.

right HERE IS A BORDER ON A STONY ALKALINE CLAY THAT HAS NEVER BEEN WATERED AND HAS TO BE DEER- AND RABBIT-PROOF. PROVING THAT THERE IS NO SUCH THING AS AN IMPOSSIBLE SITE, *ELAEAGNUS ANGUSTIFOLIA* CASPICA GROUP AND THE *CYNARA CARDUNCULUS* (CARDOON) CAST 'SHADOWS' ARTFULLY COMPOSED OF *BERBERIS THUNBERGII* AND *EUPHORBIA DULCIS* 'CHAMELEON'.

left A GRAY WAXY BLOOM ON STEMS AND LEAVES IS COMMON TO *ROSA GLAUCA* AND *IRIS GERMANICA*, ENTANGLED HERE WITH SILVERY GRAY *ARTEMISIA LUDOVICIANA* 'VALERIE FINNIS'. THE QUIET CHARM OF SUCH A TEXTURAL COMPOSITION HAS GREAT STAYING POWER, AND SETS UP THE VIEWER FOR THE CRESCENDO OF SATURATED COLORS TO COME.

right *NICOTIANA SYLVESTRIS* IS SURELY THE MOST ELEGANT OF THE TOBACCO FAMILY. HELD 5 FEET ABOVE A LARGE MASS OF LEAVES, THE FLOWERS BEGIN TO EXUDE THEIR SWEET FRAGRANCE AS EVENING FALLS. *VERBENA BONARIENSIS*, SEEN BEHIND *NICOTIANA*, IS A GOOD SELF-SEEDER AND GROWS TO A SIMILAR HEIGHT.

various rots. *Artemisia* and *Eryngium*, grown on the exposed, stony terraces at Hadspen, thrive and colonize the gravel paths and pavings, selecting cracks and crevices no gardener could hope or dare to plant. As many of the silvered plants originate in the drier Mediterranean climates, it is important to resist tidying them, cutting them back or pruning them until the spring: the debris will protect vestigial overwintering buds from damp as well as cold. It will also harbor helpful predatory insects, which will then be able to get the jump on early aphids — we also like to knot bundles of dry grass and leave them on the borders, to give winter shelter to ladybirds.

The sort of arid yet soft-edged landscape that can be created with these textural colors always looks best set against an architectural or stony background. The way brick or stone is enhanced by the superimposed concentric rings of silvery lichens is easy to overlook, yet the subtle shifts in tone could easily be taken as the basis for a fabric or interior — or a garden planting scheme. The ragged silver leaves of

Cynara cardunculus (cardoon) have an air of being carved from marble, and indeed decorate many a classical frieze. Their silvered structure stands out most beautifully against a brick or stone wall, and, as with many silvered plants, their stony color gives them a solid presence.

Of all the colored-leaved plants and shrubs, it is only the gray-leaved of which it is better to have more rather than less. Their appeal is constant, and it is hard to overdo them. The eye, once attuned to this soft color, becomes able to discern its delicate shifts of tone and quality, experiencing a phenomenon akin to *pleochroism*, the opalescent shifts seen in soap bubbles. Goethe described this complex sensation as "catotropical"; to us it is cobwebs and pearls, moonlight on waterlilies.

In a perfect world, where white flowers appear on silver foliage, as in *Convolvulus cneorum*, and gray leaves emerge from pearly stones — like *Crambe maritima* in its natural habitat — harmony reigns. Dreams here would be fulfilled by a note of discord, like the magenta bell with a yellow eye of *Gladiolus communis* ssp. *byzantinus*.

SPRING

SUMMER

AUTUMN

from top to bottom

TULIPA 'WHITE TRIUMPHATOR'

DICENTRA SPECTABILIS 'ALBA'

DAHLIA MERCKII 'ALBA'

LEUCOJUM AESTIVUM 'GRAVETYE GIANT'

IRIS ENSATA 'ALBA'

ROSA 'MARGARET MERRIL'

NOTHOSCORDUM INODORUM

BORAGO OFFICINALIS 'ALBA'

LATHYRUS LATIFOLIUS 'ALBUS'

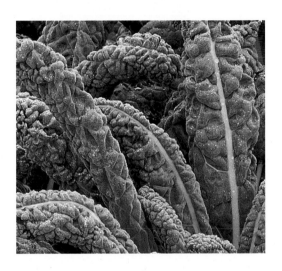

ALLIUM PORRUM

STACHYS BYZANTINA

RUBUS THIBETANUS

ARTEMISIA LUDOVICIANA 'VALERIE FINNIS'

ECHEVERIA ELEGANS

MELIANTHUS MAJOR

SEDUM SPECTABILE

BRASSICA 'CAVOLO NERO'

HELICHRYSUM ITALICUM

plant directory

This directory covers the subjects featured in the plant palette for each color. A note of the probable size (height × spread) and hardiness of the plant is followed by short cultural details, including methods of propagation. Anyone who gardens will discover that the matter of hardiness is as complex and fascinating as it is (sometimes) exasperating. The factors involved are still not completely understood, so use the figures below only as a guide.

BLUE   SPRING

Phlox divaricata 'Dirigo Ice'
herbaceous perennial
10 × 24 in.
hardy to −22°F
These low-spreading plants are clothed in flowers for many weeks. On well-drained, rich soil in part shade they spread and root as they go. Indifferent to whether the soil is acidic or alkaline, they do like the humus of leaf mold. Propagate in summer by means of cuttings taken from creeping shoots, which root readily at the nodes.

Veronica gentianoides
evergreen perennial
18 × 18 in.
hardy to −13°F
Attractive small, shiny leaves in clusters of basal rosettes mat the ground in well-drained, sunny soil; 18 in. spikes of palest blue, outward-facing flowers rise up over a long period from late spring. Propagate by taking cuttings of the many spreading stems in summer, after flowering.

Centaurea montana
(mountain knapweed)
herbaceous perennial
18 × 24 in.
hardy to −22°F
In late spring these blue explosions show well against their soft, silver-backed leaves. Grow in well-drained soil in sun; tolerant of dry, chalky soil. If cut right down after flowering, fresh leaves and some flowers will be produced in late summer. Propagate by seed or division in spring.

Camassia leichtlinii Caerulea Group
(western bluebell)
perennial bulb
48 × 8 in.
hardy to −13°F
Loving the damp, open meadows of northwestern America, these grand bulbs adapt well to pastoral or garden life. They like to be left alone to make large clumps, happy with either acid or alkaline soil as long as it does not dry out, and sun or part shade. Propagate by dividing bulbs in late summer.

Lathyrus vernus cyaneus
herbaceous perennial
15 × 12 in.
hardy to −13°F
These charming, ferny vetches are covered in small blue pea-flowers for weeks in the spring, slowly developing into an impressive clump. They prefer a sandy, well-drained soil in sun. Propagate by seed sown in spring.

Muscari armeniacum
(grape hyacinth)
perennial bulb
8 × 3 in.
hardy to −4°F
These rapidly spreading bulbs have been cultivated in gardens since Roman times. Adaptable to most soil types, they like sun and propagate themselves easily by division of their bulbs or by seed.

SUMMER

Borago laxiflora
herbaceous perennial
18 × 24 in.
hardy to −13°F
Rarely out of flower from summer to winter, with azure bells rising from rosettes of hairy leaves, several to each of the branching stems. It loves to colonize the edges of gravel paths and dry, seemingly inhospitable soil in either sun or shade. Propagated easily from seed.

Nigella damascena 'Miss Jekyll'
(love-in-a-mist)
annual
24 × 3 in.
First highly dissected, bright green, thread-like foliage adds an out-of-focus backdrop to tall subjects, then bright blue flowers, followed by bladderlike seedpods, pale brown with red. Well-drained soil in sun. Self-seeds freely, or can be propagated by seed sown at site in late winter.

Echinops bannaticus 'Taplow Blue'
(globe thistle)
herbaceous perennial
6 ft. × 6 ft.
hardy to −22°F
One of the great structural plants of the blue border. The spiky buds have a good blue-green color long before they flower, held high above deeply lobed and serrated silver-backed leaves. They need a rich, moisture-retentive soil in sun to give their best. Propagate by root cuttings in winter. Generally untroubled by pests or diseases.

Scilla peruviana
(Peruvian lily)
perennial bulb
18 × 12 in.
hardy to 10°F
A misleading common name, as these are from the Mediterranean. Fifty to a hundred starry flowers on a terminal raceme are held on a sturdy stalk. Will thrive for years if left undisturbed in well-drained soil in sun or part shade. Propagate by division of the bulbs after flowering, or by seed in spring.

Delphinium grandiflorum
herbaceous perennial
2 × 1 ft.
hardy to −22°F
Several intensely blue, rather large flowers an inch or so across, held on wiry stems of modest height, make this a very different plant from the tall delphiniums of most gardens. They will flower all summer and are excellent for cutting, which will also encourage longevity. They prefer a well-drained sunny position but do not mind alkalinity. Propagate by seed in early spring.

Salvia patens
(sage)
herbaceous perennial
24 × 18 in.
hardy to 14°F
These tuberous-rooted Mexican natives love heat and sun, and all summer and autumn will reward rich feeding with the purest blue flowers to be found in the plant world. Well worth the effort of keeping them dry in the winter. Propagate by seed in early spring, or by cuttings of new shoots in late spring.

AUTUMN

Caryopteris x clandonensis 'Heavenly Blue'
(spiraea)
deciduous shrub
3 × 2 ft.
hardy to 14°F
Narrow, faintly aromatic gray-green leaves with clusters of bright blue, tubular flowers. These are borne on new growth, so the plant can be treated to a short shearing in mid-March, but never prune in autumn. Wind and drought tolerant, it loves the sun and does well in stony ground. Propagate by softwood cuttings in early summer.

Lobelia siphilitica
(cardinal flower)
herbaceous perennial
3 × 1 ft.
hardy to −4°F
Autumnal spikes of bright blue arise from evergreen rosettes of light green leaves. It prefers damp, cool conditions, in sun or shade, and mixes admirably with Hosta and Actaea. Dividing the rosettes every spring will encourage longevity. Propagate by seed or division in early spring.

Geranium wallichianum 'Buxton's Variety'
(cranesbill)
herbaceous perennial
1 × 3 ft.
hardy to −22°F
Carries large blue, white-eyed blooms from the end of June until well after the first autumn frost. Prefers a cool, damp root run with the flowers in the sun. The wide-spreading shoots do not root, and division is difficult. Propagate by seed in spring.

Clematis heracleifolia 'Wyevale'
herbaceous shrub
3 × 4 ft.
hardy to −4°F
Pliable, 3-ft. long stems arise from a woody base, bearing clusters of fragrant hyacinthlike flowers in the axes of the upper leaves. Silky silver seedheads replace the flowers, held well into winter. Enjoys a good, moisture-retentive alkaline soil in sun or part shade. Propagate by internodal cuttings of new growth in early summer.

Ceratostigma willmottianum
(hardy plumbago)
herbaceous perennial
3 × 3 ft.
hardy to 5°F
Loves sun and fertile soil. A multitude of wiry stems carries a seemingly endless supply of bright, star-blue, plumbago-like flowers, opening one after another for months. Propagate by cuttings in late spring.

Aconitum 'Newry Blue'
(monkshood)
herbaceous perennial
5 × 2 ft.
hardy to −22°F
These stately spires with their handsome, holly-green foliage are immune to most diseases, while deer, rabbits and even slugs

leave them alone, for they are one of the most poisonous garden plants. The bulbous roots must be handled with particular caution. Moisture-retentive soil in shade or sun. Propagate by dividing roots.

GREEN SPRING

Tulipa 'Spring Green'
(Viridiflora tulip)
perennial bulb
height 18 in.
hardy to –4°F
A benevolent virus causes a variable yellow-green stripe on the petals of these wonderful tulips. Plant in clumps or drifts of 7–12 bulbs. This one seems to persist in the ground for a number of years if planted in well-drained soil in full sun; otherwise lift, dry off and store as usual.

Helleborus foetidus
(stinking hellebore)
evergreen perennial
18 × 12 in.
hardy to 5°F
The black-green foliage of this woodland plant is in striking contrast to the winter-borne, yellow-green flowers. A whiff of their scent is sweet on the winter air. Moisture-retentive soil in sun or part shade. Propagate from fresh seed sown immediately upon collection; germination will take several months. Remove old flower stalk after seed harvest.

Eryngium giganteum
(Miss Willmott's ghost)
herbaceous biennial
40 × 6 in.
hardy to –4°F
The first year's growth of bright green, shiny orbicular leaves bears little resemblance to the upright, prickly silver-gray adult plant. Propagate by sowing seed at site in the autumn. Prefers poor, dry soil in full sun.

Hosta 'Frances Williams'
(plantain lily, funkia)
herbaceous perennial
30 × 24 in.
hardy to –22°F
The grandest of variegated hostas, the broad, gold margins sometimes bleed into the blue-gray of the leaves. Heavy damp alkaline soil suits all hostas, in shade or part sun. Propagate by dividing the crown in midsummer or midwinter.

Brunnera macrophylla 'Hadspen Cream'
(Siberian bugloss)
herbaceous perennial
18 × 24 in.
hardy to –4°F
The intense forget-me-not-like flowers come in the early spring, well before borage, last longer, and never get mildew. The somewhat coarse leaves should be sheared over in early summer, to be renewed and look fresh until the autumn. Moisture-retentive rich soil in shade or part sun. Propagate this form only by division of the crown, in autumn or spring.

Lupinus 'Chandelier'
herbaceous perennial
4 × 2 ft.
hardy to –4°F
Lupins come in a useful range of colors, across the spectrum, and adapt to virtually all climates and soils, although they tend to be short-lived on heavy ground. In cool summers they can be kept flowering all season by vigorous deadheading. Propagate by division of named forms in early spring, or by seed of the various species or strains.

SUMMER

Angelica archangelica
(wild parsnip)
herbaceous biennial
7 × 3 ft.
hardy to –4°F
This imposing plant rockets to its full height in its second year, before flowering. Easily grown in full sun in any but soggy soil, it is beautiful even after it dies, making a natural 'dried' flower. Propagate by seed in early spring, sown at site if possible.

Nicotiana alata 'Lime Green'
(flowering tobacco)
tender annual
2 × 2 ft.
These floriferous plants come in various sumptuous, subtle shades, and many have a divine scent. In these green forms, the purple-blue anthers make a good contrast. Fertile soil in sun or part shade. Propagate in early spring by seed sown under glass.

Fritillaria imperialis
(crown imperial)
herbaceous bulb
40 × 12 in.
hardy to –4°F
Many bulbs and annuals have attractive seedheads, with a sculptural quality very different from any flower, lending another dimension to the garden. Sometimes, as with this fritillaria, the seedpod seems to bear no relation to the flower; if the dead leaves are removed, it will look intriguing for months. Fertile soil in sun.

Lactuca sativa 'Cocarde'
biennial
1 × 1 ft.
hardy to 34°F
Lettuce is, of course, the most common salad plant, but can be moved from the potager to the border to provide excellent foliage in a wide range of textures and colors. The copper-red types are not attacked by aphids, which do not see this color as lunch. A rich, well-drained soil in full sun grows the most luscious leaves. Propagate by seed sown where you want it to grow, throughout the summer.

Cynara cardunculus Scolymus Group
(artichoke)
herbaceous evergreen perennial
4 × 4 ft.
hardy to 14°F
This is often grown only in the vegetable garden, but its long silver leaves and 6 in.-wide blue flowers could earn it a place in any well-fed, sunny border. Tie the leaves together and tuck a straw mulch up around the base to help it winter well. Propagate by division in early spring for named forms, or by seed sown in spring.

Ficus carica 'Brown Turkey'
(fig)
deciduous shrub to small tree
10 × 20 ft.
hardy to 5°F
Beautifully lobed leaves and delectable fruit make this surprisingly hardy Mediterranean tree worthy of a choice, well-drained corner of the garden in sun or part shade. A restricted root run will increase its harvest. Propagate from summer or winter cuttings of current growth.

AUTUMN

Kniphofia 'Percy's Pride'
(red-hot poker)
herbaceous evergreen perennial
4 × 2 ft.
hardy to 14°F
Many good forms of *Kniphofia* are available, from pale green to pure orange, short, medium and tall. They enjoy good garden soil in full sun, and some protection of the crown when the weather is wet and cold. To encourage flowering, deadhead regularly and divide clumps every 3–4 years. Propagate by division in early spring.

Eucomis comosa
(pineapple lily)
bulbous perennial
24 × 18 in.
hardy to 14°F
In this tropical-looking plant, racemes of star-shaped flowers arise from a rosette of straplike, pearl-green leaves. Although hardy in many areas if planted in well-drained soil in full sun, they are also fun in an ornamental pot, where they will not need to be disturbed for many years. Propagate by dividing the bulb in winter.

Petroselinum crispum
(parsley)
herbaceous biennial
12 × 8 in.
hardy to –4°F
Long familiar in the herb garden and once the ubiquitous decoration on restaurant food, our success with it explodes the myth that you have to be bossy to grow it well. Grow in sunny, enriched soil. Propagate by seed, preferably sown at site.

Paulownia tomentosa
(foxglove tree)
deciduous tree
70 × 35 ft.
hardy to 5°F
This fast-growing tree from China, if cut down each year (as it is at Hadspen), will produce huge, juvenile leaves 30 in. across, but you will not get the pale blue foxglove-like racemes of flowers with this treatment: they are susceptible to late frosts. Propagate by seed sown in spring. Fertile, well-drained soil in sun or part shade.

Astilboides tabularis
(syn. *Rodgersia tabularis*)
herbaceous perennial
3 × 3 ft.
hardy to –20°F
A useful plant for creating a big-leaved effect. The peltate leaves have the charming characteristic of holding water in the cup thus formed. The astilbe-like white flowers arise directly from the congested rhizome. Propagate by division in late winter. Heavy, moisture-retentive soil in sun or shade.

Hosta 'Francee'
(plantain lily, funkia)
herbaceous perennial
30 × 24 in.
hardy to –40°F
One of the best white-and-green variegated forms in this overly abundant group. *Hosta* is, of course, an excellent plant for shade, or pot. The white stripe of 'Francee' does not suffer a physiological breakdown in the sun, as many others do. Moisture-retentive soil in shade or sun. Propagate by division in midsummer or midwinter.

YELLOW SPRING

Euphorbia polychroma
(spurge)
herbaceous perennial
18 × 18 in.
hardy to –4°F
An even mound of bracts on bright chartreuse terminal shoots begins to color just in time to coincide with the Viridiflora tulips, with which they look so attractive. Like that of all euphorbias, the sap is a poisonous skin irritant. They need well-drained, not rich soil, in sun. Propagate by cuttings of new growth in summer.

Primula vulgaris 'Val Horncastle'
(double primrose)
herbaceous perennial
8 × 8 in.
hardy to 5°F
In these double forms of the common primrose, the extra petals take the place of

the stamens; as they cannot be pollinated, they just keep on flowering and flowering. These floriferous small plants prefer an alkaline loam in sun or shade. Propagate by division into single rosettes, which will also keep them growing vigorously.

Dicentra spectabilis 'Goldheart'
(bleeding-heart)
herbaceous perennial
3 x 2 ft.
hardy to −31°F
This newest form of an exquisite old garden plant was selected by us at Hadspen Garden in 1993. The broad, bright yellow leaves are held on sturdy, translucent, peach-colored stems. In rich, leafy soil in semishade, 'Goldheart' will flourish until early summer, and when cut back by half, will refurbish itself with new leaves. Propagation is by tissue culture.

Fritillaria imperialis 'Maxima Lutea'
(crown imperial)
perennial bulb
40 x 12 in.
hardy to −4°F
These long-lived, freely flowering bulbs produce elegant, drooping bells on sturdy stems. They benefit from a loamy soil in full sun, where they will multiply well, and need dividing when congested. Propagate by rooting bulb scales in a frame, like lilies.

Doronicum orientale 'Magnificum'
(leopard's-bane)
herbaceous perennial
18 x 18 in.
hardy to −13°F
These cheerful, bright yellow daisies coincide perfectly with bluebells (*Scilla endymion nonscriptus*), making an ideal contrast. Very adaptable as to soil type; flowers well in conditions from full sun to full shade. Propagate by seed in spring or by division after flowering.

Tulipa 'Yokohama'
perennial bulb
height 14 in.
hardy to −22°F
The pale, Indian-yellow blooms with elegant, pointed petals are held on soft gray stems and leaves, harmonizing with the early native *Primula vulgaris*, which flowers at the same time. Prefer fertile soil in sun; persisting well in sandy soil, they otherwise need to be dug up after dying down, dried off and stored. Propagate by dividing bulbs.

SUMMER

Potentilla recta pallida
(cinquefoil)
herbaceous perennial
2 x 1 ft.
hardy to −4°F
Multiple heads of strawberrylike flowers rise up on tall, wiry stems from rosettes of

hairy leaves. Thrives and flowers well in a sunny site and prefers well-drained soil, not necessarily rich. If deadheaded will go on flowering until the autumn. Propagate by seed sown in spring.

Cephalaria gigantea
(giant scabious)
herbaceous perennial
6 x 3 ft.
hardy to −22°F
These grand herbaceous plants form huge, leafy clumps that send up tall, rigid stems bearing pale yellow disks for most of the summer. In ordinary soil in sun or shade, they thrive for years. Divide clumps in half to rejuvenate. Propagate by division in winter or by seed sown in spring.

Allium flavum
(yellow onion)
perennial bulb
14 x 2 in.
hardy to −4°F
These tiny bulbs spread easily in loose soil, sending up a multitude of wiry stems from low, sprawling foliage in an explosion of bright flowers looking for all the world like yellow sparklers. Well-drained soil in full sun. Propagate if necessary by division of the bulbs after flowering.

Anthemis tinctoria 'E.C. Buxton'
herbaceous perennial
2 x 3 ft.
hardy to −4°F
A low mound of vivid green, ferny foliage supports sheaves of clear, pale yellow daisies through the summer. Cutting down the flowers as they fade will ensure the plant's longevity and a few flowers in the autumn. Well-drained soil, not too rich, preferably in sun. Propagate by taking cuttings of the self-rooting stems.

Achillea filipendulina 'Gold Plate'
(yarrow)
herbaceous perennial
40 x 18 in.
hardy to −13°F
Forms large clumps of feathery, gray-green leaves with strong stems supporting flat, golden-yellow flowers that seem to float above the plant. Unfussy about soil type, but does not like it wet: most forms are drought tolerant, and all love the sun. Propagate by cuttings of basal shoots in late spring, or by division of the clumps.

Phlomis longifolia
(Jerusalem sage)
evergreen shrub
5 x 5 ft.
hardy to 5°F
Stiffly curved branches are covered in amber-colored felt matching the hairy covering of the long, dark, rugose leaves. Hardier than most *Phlomis* species, this one rarely loses its young growth in winter. Covered in large, golden-yellow flowers

in midsummer followed by a few through the autumn. Full sun and good drainage are essential. Propagate by nodal cuttings in midsummer.

AUTUMN

Oenothera biennis
(evening primrose)
biennial
60 x 6 in.
hardy to −13°F
Fragrance seems to exude from these stalky plants in the evening. They need a sunny site, but will grow in almost any soil, unless it is very wet, making substantial rosettes of long narrow leaves with reddish central ribs the first year, shooting to their full size in the second year. Propagate by seed sown in trays or at site.

Helianthus annuus
(sunflower)
annual
10 x 2 ft.
The fun of growing these plants has been enhanced lately by the introduction of sumptuous color forms, velvety bronzes, mahogany and peach tones, in doubles and dwarfs as well as singles and giants. A good, well-drained, sunny soil will help them do their best. Propagate by seed sown at site.

Beta vulgaris 'Golden Chard'
(Swiss chard)
biennial
2 x 2 ft.
hardy to 14°F
These stunning plants from the humble beet family are as beautiful in the garden as they are tasty on the plate. This new golden form was selected at Hadspen Garden from seeds given to us by the exciting Australian seed company, Digger's. Rich soil and a sunny position suit it. Propagate by seed sown in spring.

Helenium 'Butterpat'
(sneezeweed)
herbaceous perennial
60 x 18 in.
hardy to −13°F
These are the backbone of the late border. Form large clumps quickly, providing many divided stems of flowers with fringed silky yellow petals held away from their powdery-yellow, thimblelike centers. Well-drained, rich, fertile soil in sun. Propagate by division in early spring.

Rudbeckia hirta 'Irish Eyes'
(coneflower)
herbaceous perennial
2 x 2 ft.
hardy to −22°F
Essential plants for the autumn border and for naturalized grasslands. Branched stems rising from tufts of broad, dark green leaves hold many flowers that open over a long

period, usually until the frost. Yearly division in spring will help keep these sometimes short-lived perennials going. Fertile soil in sun. Propagate by division or seed in spring.

Rosa 'Graham Thomas'
deciduous shrub
6 x 3 ft.
hardy to −22°F
Clusters of lusciously textured, rich yellow flowers on stiff, upright stems; tea rose fragrance. This healthy modern rose is one of David Austin's best. Almost continuously in flower, it enjoys a heavy, rich soil with plenty of farmyard muck, in full sun. Prune hard in late winter.

ORANGE SPRING

Tulipa 'Golden Artist'
(Viridiflora tulip)
perennial bulb
height 1 ft.
hardy to −22°F
Flowers in mid-May. Golden-orange petals are embellished with a jade-green stripe. Plant 6 in. deep, in clumps or drifts of 7–12 bulbs, in well-drained soil in full sun, to bake in the summer, if you intend to leave bulbs at site; or lift and dry off.

Meconopsis cambrica
(Welsh poppy)
herbaceous perennial
18 x 12 in.
hardy to 5°F
An abundant colonizer and great friend of the woodland gardener. From tufts of pale green, hairy leaves arise threadlike stems carrying small, 1 in., pure-colored blooms, apparently always in motion. Damp leafy soil suits it, acidic or alkaline, in full sun or shade. Propagate by seed sown at site.

Geum 'Dolly North'
herbaceous perennial
24 x 18 in.
hardy to −4°F
Double yellow-orange flowers are held on wiry stems above clumps of green, hairy foliage that makes good ground cover. Flowers from spring to summer if individual blooms are deadheaded. Needs a rich, fertile soil in sun or part shade. Propagate this cultivar from divisions only, in spring.

Fritillaria imperialis 'The Premier'
(crown imperial)
perennial bulb
48 x 18 in.
hardy to −4°F
With an impressive cluster of rich orange bells perched on a tall, stiff stem topped with a crest of green leaves, this is best suited to the back of the border, where its dying foliage can be disguised by other plants. Plant 6 in. deep in sunny, well-drained, fertile soil.

Euphorbia griffithii 'Fireglow'
(spurge)
herbaceous perennial
3 x 2 ft.
hardy to –4°F
Orange buds emerging in early spring unfold amid green foliage edged and veined orange-red, forming intense brick-orange flowers in terminal umbels over a long period before fading into the autumn. Will spread by underground rhizomes in rich soil, in sun or part shade. Some people show a sensitivity to the sap of all spurges: wear gloves when handling.

Paeonia delavayi x *P. delavayi* var. *lutea*
(tree peony)
deciduous shrub
6 x 6 ft.
hardy to –4°F
This cross, which occurs naturally, results in amber-to-deep-orange blossoms with a thick tassel of honey-colored stamens, followed by pods of shiny black seeds. Decorative dissected foliage with good autumn color on rather gaunt, upright stems. A spring tidying of any dead leaves still hanging dejectedly on the stems is sometimes a cosmetic necessity. Fertile, well-drained soil in sun.

SUMMER

Oenothera versicolor 'Sunset Boulevard'
(evening primrose)
annual
24 x 6 in.
Almost identical to the type, with clusters of pale orange flowers maturing to brick red-orange held in whorls on red stems. Handsome green foliage with central red rib. Upright branching growth. Will flower all summer with some deadheading. Well-drained soil in sun. Propagate by seed sown under glass in spring.

Rosa 'Westerland'
(modern shrub rose)
deciduous shrub
6 x 4 ft.
hardy to –22°F
Clusters of large, bright, golden peach-orange double, scented blooms are held on stiff, upright stems carrying healthy, glossy, dark green foliage. This strong, vigorous shrub is almost continuously in flower throughout the summer, especially when deadheaded. Prune back new growth to two or three buds to shape bush in February. Needs rich soil in full sun.

Potentilla 'William Rollison'
(cinquefoil)
herbaceous perennial
18 x 18 in.
hardy to –13°F
Double orange blooms with yellow reverse on tall, branching, wiry stems flowering for a long period throughout the summer.

Clumps of dark green, strawberrylike foliage free from pests or diseases make handsome ground cover. Well-drained, fertile soil in sun. Propagates slowly, from divisions in spring.

Arctotis x *hybrida* 'Flame'
(African daisy)
half-hardy perennial
20 x 16 in.
hardy to 32°F
Terracotta flowers set off by lobed, felty gray foliage. Blooms nonstop from May to the first hard frost. Easily propagated from cuttings. An excellent plant for containers as well as in the border. Rich soil in sun — it will refuse to open on a dull day.

Zinnia species
annual
3 x 2 ft.
This charming species from Mexico flowers continuously until the late autumn. Clusters of small, flat flowers, 1 in. across, start brick red, fading to orange then to mahogany. Stiff upright, bushy, well-branched plants. Sow seed under glass in March, setting out plants after last frost. Fertile, well-drained soil in sun.

Eschscholzia californica 'Dalli'
(California poppy)
half-hardy perennial
8 x 12 in.
hardy to 14°F
Prolific silky flowers over gray-green dissected foliage. Thrives on poor soil in full sun. Will often seed into the path. Like most poppies, resents root disturbance: best to sow seed at site, or into peat pots. Other color selections have been made, in pale pink, purple and creamy yellow.

AUTUMN

Colutea x *media*
(bladder senna)
deciduous shrub
12 x 6 ft.
hardy to –4°F
Hardy shrub with gray-green pinnate leaves, with copper, pealike flowers for months, followed by large, shiny, papery brown inflated seedpods. Vigorous: will make 3 ft. of growth after pollarding back to three buds on the main stems in spring. Full sun in well-drained soil. Propagate by seed sown in spring.

Asclepias tuberosa
(butterfly weed)
herbaceous perennial
2 x 1 ft.
hardy to –4°F
Many clusters of small, bright orange flowers borne in late summer on stiff upright, furry stems clothed with pale green lanceolate leaves. Deep, sandy, very well-drained soil in full sun in a sheltered

position. Plant fleshy root 4 in. deep. In hot summers; narrow pointed pods burst with silky seed.

Dahlia 'David Howard'
half-hardy perennial tuber
3 x 2 ft.
hardy to 23°F
Amber decorative-type flower combines with shiny, dark brown leaves. Pinch out growing shoots to make a stout branching plant. Flowers from July to late autumn. In warmer localities tubers may be left in the ground over winter, but otherwise should be lifted and stored in frost-free conditions. Fertile, rich soil in full sun. Propagate by basal cuttings or division of tubers in spring.

Leonotis nepetifolia
(lion's-ear)
annual
6 x 2 ft.
A robust annual for the back of the border. Whorls of large, fuzzy, russet-colored flowers resembling *Nepeta*, are spaced at about 6-in. intervals along the stems. Raise from seed sown in March and set out in May to flower from June to late autumn. Rich, well-drained soil in full sun.

Helenium 'Moerheim Beauty'
(sneezeweed)
herbaceous perennial
3 x 2 ft.
hardy to –22°F
Richly colored, slightly reflexed, composite petals radiate from prominent brown centers with gold stamens on branching stems. Needs staking to support abundant flowers. Thrives on rich soil in sun. Divide congested clumps every 4–5 years. Flowers from July to autumn. Propagate by division or stem cuttings in spring.

Tagetes patula
(French marigold)
annual
3 x 2 ft.
Flowers of all shapes and in shades of orange, yellow, russet and brown are borne for many months, until the first hard frost. The scent of the roots and the dissected foliage acts as a deterrent to nematodes and whitefly. Grows easily from seed sown in March in a cool greenhouse for planting out in late May. Withstands both drought and rainy conditions. Prefers fertile soil and full sun.

RED SPRING

Chaenomeles speciosa
(Japanese quince)
deciduous shrub
8 x 15 ft.
hardy to –13°F
Vigorous branching, thorny stems form a large shrub that can be trained against a

wall or fence. Flowering, in bunches on last year's wood beginning before leaves appear; continues for a long period, followed by small, round, yellow fruits in autumn. Well-drained fertile soil in full sun. May be chlorotic on very limy soil.

Geum 'Mrs J. Bradshaw'
herbaceous perennial
32 x 18 in.
hardy to –4°F
Branching sprays of rounded small, double flowers on tall stems held above tight clumps of hairy, lobed, bright green leaves. Deadhead individual blooms to extend flowering period. Fertile soil in sun or part shade. Will come true from seed, or increase by division. Disease and pest free.

Tulipa praestans 'Fusilier'
perennial bulb
height 10 in.
hardy to –22°F
Unusual, with multiple stems and clusters of 3–5 flowers, rising from a sheaf of glaucous broad leaves. Plant in clumps of 7–12 bulbs. Flowers earlier than most of the hybrid tulips. Will thrive at site if they are given good drainage in full sun. Try growing them naturalized in meadow grass.

Aquilegia vulgaris var. *flore-pleno* (red)
(columbine)
herbaceous perennial
36 x 18 in.
hardy to –4°F
Elegant sprays of spurless, pomponlike, fully double flowers on stiff stems over ferny foliage tinged plum. *Aquilegia* can be promiscuous, but this one comes true from seed, seeding itself freely in the border. Well-drained, fertile soil in sun.

Paeonia delavayi
(tree peony)
deciduous shrub
6 x 4 ft.
hardy to –4°F
Gaunt upright growth, bearing handsome divided leaves tinged red. Flowers formed terminally on the stems and held by leafy bracts on reddish stalks, followed by dark, crusty pods of shiny black seeds. Contain vigorous growth by pruning out older wood in spring, and remove lingering dead leaves. Well-drained, rich soil in sun.

Viola x *wittrockiana* (red)
evergreen perennial
6 x 8 in.
hardy to 14°F
Hardy as *Viola* is, it often behaves as an annual, apparently worn out by its prolific flowering. Frequent deadheading will encourage flowering for most of the summer. Give it a cool root run in rich soil in sun or part shade. Propagate named forms by cuttings of basal shoots in July, or sow seed of selected strains in spring.

SUMMER

Potentilla 'Gibson's Scarlet'
(cinquefoil)
herbaceous perennial
18 x 24 in.
hardy to –4°F
Low mounds of healthy, green, strawberry-like leaves make excellent ground cover, while sprays of small flowers held above on thin, branching stems add a haze of color. Position where stems can clamber into supporting neighboring plants, or stake. Fertile, well-drained soil in sun. Will flower for a long period with deadheading.

Tropaeolum majus 'Red Wonder'
(nasturtium)
annual
1 x 2 ft.
Double flowers set above tight mounds of handsome, rounded, blue-green leaves. This cultivar must be propagated by cuttings. Flowers until a hard frost, often best in the cool of autumn. Rich soil in full sun. Flowers make a nice addition to a summer salad.

Hemerocallis 'Aztec'
(daylily)
herbaceous perennial
30 x 24 in.
hardy to –22°F
Fresh, pale green, straplike leaves emerge early in spring. Several flowers to each stiff stem open individually and last one day. Encourage flowering by dividing congested clumps every 4–5 years. Fertile soil in sun or part shade. Recent intensive hybridizing has resulted in a wide selection of colors.

Rosa 'Lilli Marlene'
(Floribunda rose)
deciduous shrub
30 x 24 in.
hardy to –22°F
Clusters of medium-sized, double, velvety flowers of a perfect crimson red, repeat-flowering well into the autumn. Dark green foliage sometimes affected by blackspot. Upright small bush suited to the middle or front of the border. Fertile soil in full sun.

Salpiglossis 'Chocolate Pot'
(painted-tongue)
annual
24 x 6 in.
An exciting color selection: usually the beautiful dark red, purple and blue flowers are veined yellow. Tall erect growth, branches well when pinched out as a young plant. Does not like root disturbance, so set out when young. Full sun in fertile soil. Flowers best in a dry summer. Beautiful cool greenhouse cut flower.

Dianthus barbatus Nigrescens Group
(sweet-William)
evergreen perennial
2 x 1 ft.
hardy to 5°F

Clumps of shiny, beetroot-red leaves make 4-in. mounds, above which dark velvety flowers with a spicy perfume appear as complete posies on stiff stems. Short-lived (3–4 years), but will come true from seed. Rich, well-drained soil in full sun. Makes an excellent cut flower. Propagate from seed in spring.

AUTUMN

Canna 'Roi Humbert'
herbaceous rhizome
5 x 3 ft.
hardy to 23°F
Terminal clusters of upward-facing, gladiolus-like flowers on stiff, upright stems rise from large, exotic, tropical-looking, dark bronze, unfurling leaves. *Canna* prefers a moist, fertile soil in full sun. Lift rhizomes and store in dry, frost-free conditions. Pot up and start into growth in a cool greenhouse before planting out in spring.

Ricinus communis 'Carmencita'
(castor-oil plant)
annual
5 x 3 ft.
Fast-growing, exotic, large, dark bronze, deeply lobed leaves on stout stems of the same color, with clusters of red flowers followed by spiny seedpods. Sow seed under glass in March and set out good-sized plants after frost. Fertile, well-drained soil in full sun.

Rosa rugosa
(Japanese rose)
deciduous shrub
3 x 4 ft.
hardy to –40°F
Single, fragrant white or reddish-purple flowers are followed by large, tomato-shaped seedpods, very rich in Vitamin C, which can be used to make jam or syrup. Deeply veined, bright green, healthy foliage on very prickly stems. Thrives on rather poor, sandy soil in sun.

Dahlia 'Bishop of Llandaff'
half-hardy perennial tuber
3 x 3 ft.
hardy to 23°F
Shimmering metallic, almost black, dissected foliage is as striking as the flowers. One of the first dark-leaved dahlias in cultivation. Requires well-drained soil in a sheltered position to remain at site through the winter, otherwise lift and store in frost-free conditions. Fertile soil in full sun.

Gaillardia pulchella 'Red Plume'
(blanket flower)
annual
12 x 6 in.
Fast-growing annual bearing masses of double flowers for a very long period with the encouragement of a little deadheading. Does well in both drought and wet

conditions. Rich, well-drained soil in full sun. Propagate from seed sown under glass in spring, setting out the plants in May.

Dahlia 'Arabian Night'
half-hardy tuber
4 x 3 ft.
hardy to 23°F
Decorative-type flowers over dark green, leathery leaves borne for a long period from midsummer to the first hard frost. Benefits from deadheading. Leave in place in the border if it is well-drained and sheltered, otherwise lift and store in dry, frost-free conditions. Fertile soil in full sun.

PLUM SPRING

Fritillaria meleagris
(snake's-head fritillary)
deciduous bulb
height 1 ft.
hardy to –4°F
Best grown undisturbed in meadow grass, where it will naturalize easily. Prefers well-drained, alkaline soil in sun or part shade, but must not dry out in summer. Flower colors range from variegated pinkish-plum to white, on slender stems with gray-green leaves. Native to most of Europe.

Iris germanica 'Ruby Contrast'
(bearded iris)
herbaceous rhizome
6 x 12 in.
hardy to –13°F
This medium-sized iris is suited to the front of the border in well-drained, alkaline soil in full sun. Position rhizome above ground facing south so that it will bake in the summer heat — essential for next year's flower development. Divide every 3–4 years to avoid congestion.

Tulipa 'Black Parrot'
deciduous bulb
height 18 in.
hardy to –22°F
Upward-facing, dark plum, satiny petals, feathered and fringed, borne singly on stiff stems above gray-green foliage. Plant 6 in. deep in clumps of 7–12 bulbs. Well-drained, fertile soil in full sun. Leave at site if conditions permit, otherwise lift and store dry and frost-free.

Euphorbia dulcis 'Chameleon'
(spurge)
herbaceous perennial
30 x 30 in.
hardy to –13°F
Excellent new introduction forming tight clumps of dark chocolate-maroon foliage making excellent ground cover. Darkest coloring in full sun. After flowering, cut back to encourage fresh new growth. Tolerant of drought and a wide variety of soil types. Propagate by seed or division.

Geranium phaeum
(dusky-cranesbill, mourning-widow)
evergreen perennial
30 x 18 in.
hardy to –4°F
Flowers with reflexed petals held on lax stems over mounds of soft green, lobed leaves. Makes good ground cover, especially in shade. Free of pests and diseases. Cut back foliage after flowering to encourage fresh new growth. Several other good color variants available. Fertile, well-drained soil. Propagate by division.

Helleborus torquatus Party Dress Group
evergreen perennial
1 x 1 ft.
hardy to –4°F
Clusters of dwarf double flowers, in colors ranging from pinks to a smoky haze, on upright stems. Remove old leaves in late autumn to display the flowers better and inhibit the spread of blackspot to new leaves. Introduced by Robin White of Blackthorn Nursery. Rich, heavy soil, but not waterlogged/part shade.

SUMMER

Astrantia major 'Hadspen Blood'
(masterwort)
herbaceous perennial
36 x 18 in.
hardy to –4°F
This cross was made at Hadspen by us in 1988. Multiple flowerheads of dark crimson held by near-black bracts on upright stems from May until October. Needs fertile, rich soil in sun to color best. Excellent cut flowers. Propagation by division only.

Papaver orientale 'Patty's Plum'
herbaceous perennial
3 x 2 ft.
hardy to –22°F
An abundance of stout stems produce large, sumptuous flowers borne well above generous mounds of hairy foliage. This poppy tends to sprawl, so support with stakes well before stems appear. Cut stems and foliage to the ground after flowering, when the plant goes into dormancy. Fill the gap with annuals, or situate at back of border. Fertile, well-drained soil in sun.

Rosa 'Louis XIV'
(China rose)
deciduous shrub
3 x 2 ft.
hardy to 23°F
Semi-double, medium-sized, velvety flowers with a wonderful perfume. Dark green foliage tinged crimson. Continuous flowering. These slightly tender roses are well suited to growing in a container and spending winter in a sun room or cool greenhouse, where they will often flower at Christmas. Prune hard in the spring and lightly in midsummer. Rich soil in a hot, sunny place.

Hemerocallis 'Little Grapette'
(daylily)
herbaceous perennial
15 x 24 in.
hardy to 5°F
Branched clusters of charming smallish flowers on stout stems are produced over a long period, each one lasting a day, emerging from tidy clumps of semi-evergreen, pale green, grasslike foliage. Perfect for the front of the border, or in a small garden. Needs a rich, moist, fertile soil in full sun to flower at its best.

Allium atropurpureum
deciduous bulb
height 3 ft.
hardy to 14°F
Tall stems hold single globular heads each encased in a membrane that bursts open to reveal a cluster of dark plum, starlike flowers with purple stamens. Rather insignificant gray-green leaves appear briefly before dying away after flowering. Well-drained soil in full sun. Perfect coming through light herbaceous plants or shrubs.

Papaver somniferum 'Double Black'
(opium poppy)
annual
30 x 6 in.
A seed strain selected for its large double flowers on tall, gray-green stems clothed in large glaucous leaves. Decorative seedpods follow and will disperse thousands of seeds into the border. Dislikes root disturbance: sow at site throughout the spring and summer to establish a succession of flowering. Well-drained soil in full sun.

AUTUMN

Bracteantha bracteata 'Crimson Violet'
(strawflower)
annual
36 x 6 in.
Stiff, upright plants with branching stems carry masses of flowers for a long period, flowering from side shoots if deadheaded. They are usually grown for dried flower arrangements, but the long-lasting blooms make an interesting addition to the border. Propagate by means of seed sown under glass in spring; plant out after danger of frost. Well-drained soil in sun.

Tricyrtis formosana
(toad lily)
herbaceous perennial
30 x 18 in.
hardy to –4°F
Unusual waxy, orchidlike flowers borne in loose sheafs atop branching upright stems over shining, ribbed, dark green leaves. Underground rhizomes form a substantial clump. Fertile, rich, moisture-retentive soil in sun or part shade. Propagate by division or seed sown in spring.

Angelica gigas
biennial
6 x 2 ft.
hardy to –4°F or less
A recent introduction from Korea and Japan. Umbels 5 in. wide of shiny, plum-black flowers emerge from plum, pouchlike leaf sheaths on thick stems. Large, shining green leaves. Rich, moist soil in sun. Does not appear to seed as freely as *Angelica archangelica*, the garden angelica or wild parsnip.

Cosmos atrosanguineus
(chocolate plant)
herbaceous tuber
24 x 18 in.
hardy to 23°F
Beautiful velvety flowers like small, single dahlias hover on wiry stems above dark green foliage. Smells of the best Belgian chocolate. Excellent in a container or in the border, planted 6 in. deep in fertile, well-drained soil in full sun. Place a cloche over it in winter to keep it dry. Does not start sprouting until late May.

Sanguisorba officinalis
(great burnet)
herbaceous perennial
4 x 2 ft.
hardy to –13°F
Masses of small, brownish-maroon, bottle brush flowers are borne on thin, branched stems over clumps of attractive mid-green, pinnate foliage. Rich, fertile, moist soil in sun. Meadows and wet grassy stream sides are this plant's natural habitat in the northern hemisphere. Lovely in the late autumn border when frosted.

Pelargonium 'Dark Venus'
(geranium)
evergreen perennial
2 x 2 ft.
hardy to 34°F
Best suited to a conservatory, or to containers put out in summer. This South African native enjoys full sun, drought and fertile soil, and will flower continuously in these conditions if deadheaded regularly. Propagate by means of cuttings taken from spring through to autumn.

PINK SPRING

Malus domestica 'Golden Russet'
deciduous tree
30 x 30 ft.
hardy to –31°F
Clusters of scented, blush-pink apple blossoms are a spring delight, before the flush of bright green foliage of summer and the delicious fruits of autumn. Quick growth and easy maintenance make most fruit trees as great an asset to the border as to the orchard or kitchen garden. Rich, fertile soil in full sun.

Tulipa 'Bellflower'
(fringed tulip)
herbaceous bulb
height 2 ft.
hardy to –22°F
Interesting crystalline-edged, delicate pink petals make this an unusual and beautiful tulip. Position it to be admired closely — good in a container. Plant in good-sized clumps of 7–12 bulbs, 5–6 in. deep in fertile, well-drained soil in sun. Leave bulbs at site or lift, dry and store in frost-free conditions.

Darmera peltata
(umbrella plant)
herbaceous perennial
3 x 2 ft.
hardy to –4°F
Large drumsticklike flower clusters appear on rigid stems from a mat of thick, bright green, reptilian rhizomes. Large, shining, umbrellalike leaves follow after flowering. Marginal water plant, excellent for holding a bank as the creeping rhizomes knit together to form a mat. Moist, rich soil in shade or sun. Good autumn leaf color.

Aquilegia vulgaris 'Nora Barlow'
(columbine)
herbaceous perennial
24 x 18 in.
hardy to –13°F or less
Many double spurless pompons of green and pink are borne on stiff branching stems above elegant divided leaves. Seeds true to type through the border. Cut back stems and foliage after flowering (often a small green worm will do this for you) to encourage fresh new growth. Good soil, well-drained, in sun or part shade.

Dicentra spectabilis
(bleeding-heart)
herbaceous perennial
24 x 18 in.
hardy to –4°F or less
Dainty, heart-shaped flowers dangle along arching stems above fresh green dissected foliage. Rich, fertile soil, moist but not waterlogged, in sun or partial shade. Propagate by dividing fleshy underground rhizomes in spring.

Helleborus orientalis
(Lenten rose)
evergreen perennial
18 x 24 in.
hardy to 5°F
Branched stems of exquisite substantial flowers in a wide range of colors, from white, yellowish and pink to maroon, with or without spots, flowering for a long period. Remove old leaves in late autumn to prevent blackspot spreading to new foliage. Excellent ground cover, thriving in heavy rich soil in sun or partial shade. Plants can be divided, but resent such disturbance; best grown from fresh seed sown when ripe, usually in June or July.

SUMMER

Rosa 'Felicia'
(hybrid musk rose)
evergreen shrub
4 x 4 ft.
hardy to –4°F
Clusters of medium-sized, scented, fully double flowers on arching stems with dark green, glossy, disease-free foliage. Flowers repeatedly throughout the summer, with an excellent autumn finale. Fertile soil, well-drained, in full sun. Responds to hard pruning — back to two buds on the thick stems of last year's growth.

Geranium sanguineum var. *striatum*
(bloody cranesbill)
herbaceous perennial
12 x 18 in.
hardy to –4°F
Masses of pretty, upward-facing flowers borne singly over a long period on stems over a low hummock of dark green, deeply divided foliage. Good autumn leaf color. Likes fertile, well-drained soil in full sun. Propagate by division.

Convolvulus althaeoides
(pink bindweed)
herbaceous perennial
height 6 in.
hardy to 5°F
Open, upward-facing flowers on thin twining stems combine with gray-green, dissected foliage. Spreads happily by running underground roots, once settled, while stems clamber up and over neighboring plants. Be careful: juvenile foliage is green and distinctly different from mature summer foliage. Well-drained soil in full sun. Good in a container. Less thuggish than its hedgerow cousin.

Leuzea centauroides
herbaceous perennial
3 x 2 ft.
hardy to –4°F
Large, thistlelike, dark pink flowers 2 in. across emerge from buds of decorative, brown papery bracts on stiff, upright stems above clumps of grayish-white-lobed leaves. Well-drained limy soil in sun. Propagate by division or seed.

Rosa gallica 'Versicolor'
(Gallica rose)
deciduous shrub
3 x 3 ft.
hardy to –22°F
Large, semidouble, scented flowers with splashes of pink and white on a light crimson background and yellow stamens, flowering for a long period. Prickly stems on a robust bush with healthy foliage. Also known as *Rosa mundi*, named (according to legend) after Fair Rosamund, mistress of Henry II. Rich, fertile soil in full sun. Prune out last year's flowering stems to where new growth is visible.

Lychnis coronaria
(dusty miller)
semi-evergreen herbaceous perennial
24 x 18 in.
hardy to 5°F
Old cottage garden plant with soft, gray leaves forming woolly rosettes. Magenta-pink flowers borne on felty, branched stems over a long period. Seeds moderately in the border. Well-drained, rather poor soil in full sun. Dislikes winter wet. Often treated as a biennial.

AUTUMN

Phlox paniculata 'Mother of Pearl'
herbaceous perennial
4 x 2 ft.
hardy to −13°F
Scented panicles of many florets atop stiff upright stems clothed in green leaves. Pinch out thin shoots and half the thicker shoots in spring to ensure a succession of flowers over a long period. Moisture-retentive, rich soil in sun or part shade. Raised by Alan Bloom of Bressingham Gardens, Norfolk.

Saponaria officinalis 'Rubra Plena'
(soapwort)
herbaceous perennial
height 30 in.
hardy to −4°F
A double form of the soapwort. Its leaves make a lather used by conservators in the cleaning of fragile tapestries and other fabrics. Somewhat invasive. Cut back in late spring to encourage branching. Well suited to areas of grass or other rough land. Well-drained soil in full sun.

Anemone hupehensis 'Hadspen Abundance'
(Japanese anemone)
herbaceous perennial
24 x 18 in.
hardy to 5°F
Eric Smith, nurseryman at Hadspen in the 1970s, found this cultivar growing here. It produces an abundance of flowers with three pale pink and two dark pink petals. Dark green, deeply divided leaves. Fertile, moisture-retentive soil in sun or shade.

Hibiscus syriacus
deciduous shrub
7 x 3 ft.
hardy to −4°F
Upright twiggy shrub with dark green, three-lobed leaves and many large, trumpet-shaped flowers. Fertile, well-drained soil in full sun — the hotter the situation, the better the flowering. A valuable shrub for the late autumn border, with cultivars in a wide range of colors.

Rosa 'Zéphirine Drouhin'
(Bourbon rose)
deciduous shrub
10 x 6 ft.
hardy to −4°F
Grow this if only for its delicious perfume. Semidouble flowers are borne almost continuously on nearly thornless stems. New growth is tinged red. Can be a martyr to mildew, so ensure it has good air circulation and a humus-rich soil in full sun.

Salvia involucrata 'Hadspen'
herbaceous perennial
3 x 3 ft.
hardy to 5°F
This stoloniferous sage with handsome, smooth, scented leaves was selected for its extended, graceful bract of flowers. It will colonize a well-drained, sunny soil and bloom well into autumn when planted against a wall or building. Propagate by nodal cuttings in midspring.

PEACH SPRING

Iris germanica 'Edward of Windsor'
(tall bearded iris)
herbaceous rhizome
36 x 18 in.
hardy to −13°F
Buff-peach flowers with an apricot beard. Thrives on alkaline soil in full sun, the rhizomes situated just on top of the soil facing south, to bake in the sun and ensure next year's flowering. Propagate by dividing rhizomes in August.

Lonicera caprifolium
(honeysuckle)
deciduous climber
height 10 ft.
hardy to −4°F
Fragrant, peach-pink flowers fade to creamy buff. Twining stems are clad in perfoliate, gray-green leaves. Fertile, rich soil in full sun. Prune out flowered wood in summer. Propagate by nodal cuttings in midsummer.

Tulipa 'Apricot Parrot'
perennial bulb
height 18 in.
hardy to −22°F
Delicate salmon-pink petals with a slightly darker shading combine with gray-green leaves. Plant in clumps in well-drained soil in full sun. Leave at site if conditions are favorable, otherwise lift when foliage dies down and store in a dry, frost-free place. Propagate by division of bulbs in autumn.

Potentilla fruticosa 'Daydawn'
(shrubby cinquefoil)
deciduous shrub
3 x 3 ft.
hardy to −4°F
Many small, saucer-shaped, peach to yellow flowers over a long period, with small, green, pinnate leaves. Shape into a mound by shearing in early spring. Free from pests or diseases. Fertile, well-drained soil, but not dry, in slight shade to stop flowers fading. Propagate by softwood cuttings in summer.

Actinidia deliciosa
(kiwi fruit)
deciduous climber
height 35 ft.
hardy to 5°F
Vigorous, furry, red twining stems; grown usually for its delicious fruit, but first produces clusters of saucer-shaped apricot flowers with prominent amber stamens. Large, handsome, hairy, heart-shaped leaves. Male and female plants required for pollination. Fruits well in a hot summer. Fertile, well-drained soil in full sun.

Lupinus 'Peach'
herbaceous perennial
3 x 2 ft.
hardy to −22°F
Dense, upright spires, flowering over a long period, especially if deadheaded. Plants are often short-lived and need dividing every 3–4 years, after flowering. Propagation by seed may result in interesting color strains, but named cultivars or color selections must be increased by division. Fertile soil in full sun. Generally pest and disease free.

SUMMER

Alcea rugosa
(hollyhock)
herbaceous perennial
5 x 1 ft.
hardy to −4°F or less
Tall spires clothed in peach to yellow flowers. Deeply lobed leaves are somewhat resistant to rust. Well-drained soil in full sun. A short-lived perennial that can be propagated by seed or from basal cuttings in spring. Will seed happily in the border.

Rosa 'Alchemist'
deciduous shrub
12 x 8 ft.
hardy to −13°F
Can be grown as a climber or large shrub; here at Hadspen we train its long shoots onto hoops, encouraging the production all along their length of a profusion of extraordinary double, quartered, scented blooms. Flowers do best in a hot summer. Very healthy, leathery dark green foliage. Prefers a rich, fertile soil in sun.

Macleaya microcarpa 'Kelway's Coral Plume'
(plume poppy)
herbaceous perennial
7 x 3 ft.
hardy to 5°F or less
An architectural plant that seldom needs staking, grown for its great height and handsome foliage. Tall spires of feathery coral flowers on stems clothed in large, lobed, gray-green leaves. Spreads by fleshy underground roots and can be invasive. Well-drained soil in full sun. Propagate by division in spring or root cuttings in winter. Beware of the yellowish-orange sap, that can stain hands and clothing.

Malvastrum lateritium
herbaceous perennial
4 x 36 in.
hardy to 14°F
Charming hibiscus-shaped peach flowers borne over a long period. Makes a low, sprawling ground cover of shiny, dark green lobed leaves. A good climber against a wall, too, where it enjoys the extra warmth. Fertile, well-drained soil in full sun. Propagate by softwood cuttings in spring.

Papaver orientale 'Cedric Morris'
herbaceous perennial
3 x 2 ft.
hardy to −4°F or less
Large buff-peach flowers with maroon centers; smaller than some of the other cultivars, so staking is unnecessary. Fertile, well-drained soil in sun. Dies back after flowering, so cut back to ground level, filling the gap with annuals and half-hardy plants. Propagate by root cuttings after flowering.

Verbascum 'Helen Johnson'
(mullein)
herbaceous perennial
2 x 1 ft.
hardy to 14°F
Furry gray-green spires clad in outward-facing flowers of an unusual muddy peach rise from rosettes of soft gray-green leaves. Prune out flowered stems to prolong blooming for many weeks. Very well-drained soil (especially in winter), in full sun. Propagate by root cuttings in winter or stem cuttings in late spring.

AUTUMN

Callistephus chinensis 'Apricot Giant'
(China aster)
annual
3 x 1 ft.
Large, double blooms on stiff, upright plants that branch well if pinched back in youth. Vigorous, healthy plants may succumb to wilt. Excellent as cut flowers and as pot plants in a cool greenhouse. Fertile soil in full sun. Sow seed in spring under glass.

Kniphofia 'Apricot'
(red-hot poker)
herbaceous perennial
4 x 2 ft.
hardy to 14°F
Another terrific plant bred by Eric Smith, former nurseryman at Hadspen, forming a large, free-blooming clump in rich, fertile, free-draining soil in sun. Best protected by placing a twist of straw around the crowns in a cold winter. Propagation is slow, by division in early spring.

Hemerocallis 'Children's Festival'
(daylily)
herbaceous perennial
2 x 1 ft.
hardy to −22°F

Clusters of medium-sized flowers which open and last for one day, on stiff stems held above tight clumps of thin, straplike leaves. Fresh chartreuse foliage appears early in spring. Fertile, rich soil in sun or part shade. Propagate by division of clumps in early spring.

Potentilla x hopwoodiana
(cinquefoil)
herbaceous perennial
18 x 24 in.
hardy to 5°F
This plant has large strawberrylike flowers that keep coming all summer and autumn, even after a light frost. Plants enjoy good soil in full sun. Unlike strawberries, they do not root from their many runners but must be propagated by division of the crowns in late winter.

Helianthus annuus
(sunflower)
annual
10 x 2 ft.
Very fast-growing, with stout stalks, huge coarse leaves and gigantic flowers. Taller varieties need staking. Fertile soil in full sun. Sow seed at site for best results; pinch out growing tips to encourage branching. Birds love to eat the seeds, so leave old flower-heads and stalks in place for the winter.

Dahlia sherffii x D. coccinea 'Amber'
perennial tuber
5 x 3 ft.
hardy to –4°F
Here is a new strain of garden dahlias from Hadspen with ephemeral flowers that begin opening in early summer, continuing until late autumn. Tall, wiry, branched stems hold the blooms well above healthy foliage, making a large back-of-the-border plant. Fertile soil in sun. Good drainage and deep planting, 1 ft., is the secret of longevity and hardiness. Propagate by division of the large woody tubers or, better, by basal cuttings in spring.

WHITE SPRING

Tulipa 'White Triumphator'
(lily-flowered tulip)
perennial bulb
height 2 ft.
hardy to –13°F
An elegant, late-flowering tulip with a strong constitution. Its pure white flowers are long and waisted, with pointed and reflexed petals. Fertile, well-drained soil in sun. Best dug up and divided in summer, replanting the largest bulbs in late autumn.

Leucojum aestivum 'Gravetye Giant'
(summer snowflake)
perennial bulb
height 28 in.
hardy to –22°F

Preferring a damp or heavy soil and sun, these April-flowering bulbs like to be planted deep, 6 in., and left alone to form impressive clumps. No pests seem to bother them. Propagated by division of the bulbs in summer.

Nothoscordum inodorum
perennial bulb
height 2 ft.
hardy to –4°F or less
This rapidly spreading bulb has an odd fragrance of incense and is very useful under shrubs and roses. The tops should be pulled off after flowering to curb its increase. An indestructible plant, tolerant of drought and most soils, which rabbits, deer and slugs leave alone. Propagate, if necessary, by division of the bulbs.

Allium porrum
(leek)
biennial bulb
height 3 ft.
hardy to 14°F
Although usually relegated to the vegetable garden, few of the *Allium* tribe have finer flowers or more impressive gray leaves. Deep planting in a rich soil in sun will give the most dramatic results with this pest-free plant. The variety 'Saint Victor' has burgundy shafts with gray leaves. All leeks are propagated by means of seed sown in spring to flower the next year.

Artemisia ludoviciana 'Valerie Finnis'
(western mugwort)
herbaceous perennial
2 x 2 ft.
hardy to –4°F
This plant produces a spreading thicket of silver-gray stems. If it is cut to the ground just before it flowers (they are an insignificant yellow) it will recover within two weeks to look fresh and silvery again. Very tolerant of lime, it is also rabbit-, deer-, and slug-proof. Prefers a well-drained, sunny situation.

Sedum spectabile
herbaceous perennial
18 x 18 in.
hardy to –4°F
Sedums are often grown for their crimson ('September Glow') to green-white ('Iceberg') autumnal flowers, so popular with butterflies, but the fleshy, drought-tolerant, glaucous gray leaves are beautiful throughout spring and summer. They prefer full sun in a well-drained soil. Propagate in late spring by cuttings or division.

SUMMER

Dicentra spectabilis 'Alba'
(bleeding-heart, lady's-locket)
herbaceous perennial
24 x 18 in.
hardy to –4°F

Lifting arching, drooping sprays of crystal white, heart-shaped flowers above hummocks of ferny foliage, this plant looks so delicate but is hardy and long-lived in a leafy soil or under trees. Propagate in early spring by means of root cuttings, division of the brittle, fleshy roots, or even seed.

Iris ensata 'Alba'
(Japanese iris)
perennial rhizome
36 x 18 in.
hardy to –4°F
Selections of these most sought-after iris (formerly *I. kaempferi*) were being made in Japan as long ago as the seventeenth century. The flattened, foppish petals are held above long, bright green, grassy foliage, each leaf with a distinct rib in its center. They need damp, lime-free soil, and may be propagated by division in early September.

Borago officinalis 'Alba'
herbaceous annual
24 x 18 in.
This hardy annual self-seeds in the most inhospitable soil and into the cracks in paths. The glasslike spicules clothing the calyx, stems and leaves turn them a hoary white. Like the blue-flowered type plant, a sprig adds a hint of cucumber to a glass of gin or Pimm's. Sun or part shade. Propagate by seed sown at site or in individual pots.

Stachys byzantina
(lamb's-ears, -tails or -tongues)
evergreen perennial
2 x 3 ft.
hardy to –13°F
Planted in a sunny, well-drained position the woolly leaves, stems and flowering stalks of this well-known plant make a dense mat. It is hardy and drought tolerant, and easily propagated by means of the self-rooting side-shoots in autumn or spring.

Echeveria elegans
half-hardy perennial
6 x 12 in.
hardy to 23°F
Looking like wildly oversized *Sempervivum*, *Echeveria* makes perfectly semicircular rosettes of a glaucous gray and is stunning in a terra-cotta pot; protect it from the wet in winter. The drooping flowers in a delicate shade of coral are borne on 2 ft. stems. Grow in well-drained soil in sun. Propagate by dividing the rosettes in spring.

Brassica 'Cavolo Nero'
(black Tuscan cabbage)
evergreen biennial
3 x 1 ft.
hardy to 14°F
As tasty as it is ornamental, this member of the brassica family presents its bouquet of darkly glaucous, well-puckered leaves from summer on through all but the meanest winters. Fertile, well-drained soil in full sun. Propagate by seed sown in late spring.

Dahlia merckii 'Alba'
perennial tuber
40 x 24 in.
hardy to –4°F
This species of dahlia is amazingly hardy if planted deeply in well-drained soil; it enjoys sunshine. The delicate flowers suspended on long wiry stems seem never to be still. Propagate a specific form by rooting new basal shoots in spring, or sow seed, selecting desired forms, as we do here.

Rosa 'Margaret Merril'
(Floribunda rose)
deciduous shrub
4 x 3 ft.
hardy to –22°F
Curvaceous, satin-white petals with a blush of pink at the base and fragrant centers. Prefers rich, heavy soil in full sun.

Lathyrus latifolius 'Albus'
(perennial pea)
herbaceous perennial climber
height 6 ft.
hardy to –4°F
This excellent, drought-tolerant scrambler should be planted to droop over low walls, banks or shrubs. Tolerant of lime and poor soil in full sun, but rabbits love to munch it. Propagate by seed sown in spring.

Rubus thibetanus
deciduous shrub
6 x 6 ft.
hardy to –4°F or less
Grown for its ghostly, thorny white stems. Prune just like a raspberry (a close relative) — that is, cut away all year-old growth. Fairly tolerant of all soils from heavy alkaline clay to acidic gravel, in sun or part shade. Propagate by means of suckers.

Melianthus major
(honey flower)
herbaceous perennial
6 ft. x 3 ft.
hardy to 14°F
This South African plant has the choicest of pinnate gray leaves, but will only produce its mahogany flowers in a Mediterranean-type climate, on two-year-old growth. In cool climates it is best mulched with straw in autumn and cut to the ground in spring. Well-drained soil in full sun. Propagate by seed, or by cuttings in late spring.

Helichrysum italicum
(curry bush)
evergreen shrub
3 x 2 ft.
hardy to 5°F
A small, silvery gray Mediterranean shrub, distinctly scented of curry, but not to be used in your favorite recipe. If pruned hard in March it can be kept to a neat shape. Well-drained soil in full sun. Propagated easily by cuttings in early summer.

index

Authors' acknowledgments

To our children, Shanahan and Dorian, for all their years of understanding and indulging our passion for gardening. Family and friends, for their encouragement and support. Niall Hobhouse, for sharing his home, Hadspen, and his generous and aesthetic appreciation. Clive and Jane Nichols, to whom we are most grateful for their enthusiasm, skill and, of course, fantastic photography; they forced us into this book project and are still our friends! Everyone at Conran Octopus who worked hard to make this book possible, especially our managing editor, Richard Atkinson. Vanessa Courtier, for her most brilliant art direction. Liz Robinson, who worked miracles with the tangle of words and random thoughts with which we provided her. Jamie Compton, for his expertise and pursuit of all things horticultural and botanical. Ed Brooks, for letting us use his original drawing as the basis of our garden plan. Customers, colleagues and all the people over the years who have helped in the creation of Hadspen Garden.

Publisher's acknowledgments

The publisher wishes to thank the following illustrators, photographers and agencies for their kind permission to reproduce the photographs and artwork in this book:

10 left Albright Knox Gallery, Buffalo, New York (Gift of Seymour H. Knox, 1956. Mark Rothko, Orange and Yellow, 1956, oil on canvas, 91 x 71in., ©Kate Rothko Prizel & Christopher Rothko/DACS 1998); 12 left Appears courtesy of Blue Note Records, a division of Capitol Records, Inc. (Photograph Francis Wolff/Design by Reid Miles); 13 right Vaughan Fleming/Science Photo Library; 16–17 artwork by Katy Hepburn; 55 Nori Pope; 76 top middle Nori Pope; 131 Nori Pope.

Captions for the detail photographs at the beginning of the color chapters
18–19 Delphinium 'Alice Artindale'
20–1 Salvia patens, Corydalis flexuosa 'Père David', Lathyrus sativus
32–3 Crocosmia 'Lucifer' (foliage)
34–5 Euphorbia characias, Helianthus annuus, Cyperus longus
46–7 Cucurbita pepo
48–9 Anthemis tinctoria 'E. C. Buxton', Crocosmia 'Citronella' x, Solidago 'Goldenmosa'
62–3 Papaver orientale 'Saffron'
64–5 Phygelius x rectus, Kniphofia cultivar, Dahlia 'David Howard'
78–9 Papaver orientale 'Beauty of Livermere'
80–1 Crocosmia 'Lucifer', Knautia macedonica, Lobelia 'Fan Deep Red'
94–5 Rosa 'Louis XIV'
96–7 Cotinus coggygria 'Royal Purple', Astrantia major 'Hadspen Blood', Scabiosa 'Chile Black', Lathyrus odoratus 'Wiltshire Ripple'
108–9 Rosa 'Gertrude Jekyll'
110–11 Cleome hassleriana, Papaver orientale 'Diana', Geranium 'Ann Folkard'
124–5 Dahlia 'Ellen Shone'
126–7 Rosa 'Sally Holmes', Hemerocallis 'Children's Festival', Lupinus 'Peach'
138–9 Romneya coulteri
140–1 Plectranthus argentatus, Nicotiana sylvestris, Clematis x eriostemon 'Hendersonii', Eryngium giganteum